Gladys Taber
Still Cove Journal

Edited and with an Introduction by Constance Taber Colby

Drawings by Georgia Dearborn

1817

HARPER & ROW, PUBLISHERS, New York,
Cambridge, Hagerstown, Philadelphia, San Francisco,
London, Mexico City, São Paulo, Sydney

This book is based on a series of weekly articles by Gladys Taber that appeared as "Still Cove Sketches" in the *Cape Cod Oracle* in 1978, 1979, and 1980.

Designer: C. Linda Dingler

Library of Congress Cataloging in Publication Data

Taber, Gladys Bagg, 1899–
    Still Cove journal.
    "Based on a series of weekly articles by Gladys
Taber that appeared as 'Still Cove sketches' in the
Cape Cod oracle in 1978, 1979, and 1980."
    1. Taber, Gladys Bagg, 1899–   —Homes and haunts
—Massachusetts—Orleans. 2. Cape Cod. 3. Authors,
American—20th century—Biography. I. Colby,
Constance Taber, 1927–   . II. Title.
PS3539.A136Z527   1981   818'.5209 [B]   80–8220
ISBN 0–06–014227–8

---

82 83 84 85 10 9 8 7 6 5 4

Introduction

Constance Taber Colby

Even after I had crossed the Sagamore Bridge, high above the glitter of water that separates Cape Cod from the mainland of Massachusetts, I had no premonition—or none that I can remember, none of the vague uneasiness which is my usual forewarning of trouble.

I do remember that the drive—one I have made many times—was especially quiet that February afternoon. The Mid-Cape Highway, jammed with cars in summer and on holiday weekends, was almost deserted. The pale gold of dried winter grass set off the dark pines on either side of the highway. I also remember the sky, clear but strangely colorless. A single bird, too far away to identify, curved for a moment against the horizon and then disappeared.

My chief concern as I approached the Orleans exit was time. I was behind schedule. When I had called her the night before, Gladys had said firmly, "Now, do try to get here by five. I thought we'd have supper at Barley Neck, and it's usually crowded by six." I had smiled at that. The Barley Neck Inn, I knew, took reservations, but my mother would never dream of calling for one. It made her uncomfortable to walk past a waiting line of hungry people to a table saved just for her. And besides, she would have had to use the telephone—something she never willingly attempted except in dire emergencies, as when the dishwasher flooded the kitchen or when she saw out the window that a fishing boat had overturned during an unexpected squall.

"Don't worry," I had reassured her. "I'll be there at least by five, if not before."

But on my way north from New York, I had stopped off in Connecticut to spend the night at Stillmeadow, the family farmhouse, and somehow I had overslept. Now it was already four forty-five. I could imagine my mother, dressed for the occasion in her new rose-and-lilac silk blouse, enthroned on the sofa with a warmly dozing cat on her lap, her gold wrist-watch (which she never liked to wear) ticking on the table beside her. "Never mind, Amber," she would be saying to the small sleeper. "She'll be here any minute."

Gladys had been hospitalized twice with cancer during the previous year, but each time she recovered quickly and returned home to the small, grey-shingled house overlooking the salt inlet known locally as Mill Pond. When we had visited her there over Christmas, she seemed fine.

As I turned down the home road I looked across to Nauset Beach, where a winter surf reflected the last rays of the sun. Too bad that sunset came so early in February: it would be dark by the time we finished dinner. All the same, my mother might like to drive over to Rock Harbor and look at the water. Perhaps there would be a moon.

From force of habit I slowed down near the cluster of bayberry and beach-plum bushes at the corner, in case the small brown rabbit who lived underneath should decide, as he usually did, that the sound of an approaching car made it absolutely necessary for him to dash across the road. Then I remembered that by this time of year he would have moved to winter quarters in the woods.

That rabbit was probably the only member of the wildlife community who did not depend on handouts from Gladys. Every kind of bird, from finches to quail, plus squirrels, raccoons, opossums, and even a skunk, turned up at the door without fail. Come to think of it, the rabbit had been known to snack on the clover and mint in the front yard occasionally. "Just be glad Gram doesn't feel responsible for feeding all the local spiders too!" my younger daughter, Anne, said once as she carried a red plastic bowl of table scraps out to the yard.

"She does feed the wasps," her sister, Alice, pointed out. And it was true: the grapefruit halves impaled on the roof of the bird feeder and on the nearby fencepost were intended for the cardinals to share with the red squirrel, but in summer they were always black with wasps.

Gladys was unperturbed by teasing. "Nobody ever leaves this house feeling hungry," she would say firmly.

Once past the rabbit corner, I glanced at my watch. Exactly five o'clock—not too bad. All in all, it had been an unusually easy trip.

I was surprised to see two cars parked in my mother's driveway, although I recognized them as belonging to her close neighbors and dear friends, Olive and the pair I always thought of jointly as Gail-and-Jan. I knew that, ever since Gladys's last illness, one or another of the neighbors had made a point of dropping in at Still Cove for at least a brief visit every day—but not, as a rule, at a time when some member of the family was expected.

Now Gail came bolting out of the house. She was very pale. "You'll have to park over behind the garage," she said. "We need to leave room for the ambulance."

The little house seemed as peaceful as always, its weathered shingles silvery in the ebbing light. The air smelled of salt water and hearth smoke.

"We were hoping so much that you'd get here before the Emergency Squad arrived." Gail went on. "It's her heart."

As she held the door for me, I saw that part of my imagined scene had been correct: my mother was seated in her favorite corner just at I had pictured her, but she was still wearing her old blue robe. Amber was pacing along the back of the sofa.

When Gladys spoke to me, her voice was almost a whisper. "Your trip?" she said.

"It was fine," I said, hearty with nervousness. "Fine. No traffic." I went over to give her a hug. "How *are* you?" I asked. It was not, I realized, a very good question. I turned to the others. "Tell me what happened."

At that moment three tall young men from the fire department rescue squad loomed in the doorway with stretcher and oxygen. I heard the story as it was explained to them: the palpitations, the reluctant call to Olive ("I do hate to bother you on a Saturday—"), Dr. Bill's visit, the rapid worsening of Gladys's condition, another call to the doctor, his decision that hospital treatment was needed at once.

"You go with her in the ambulance," Jan suggested to me. "The three of us will follow in my car. I'll just telephone Helen and Vicky to come over and stay with Amber. Or if I can't reach them, I'll get Linda."

And so, swiftly and smoothly, the neighborhood network, that had sustained not only Gladys but many others who lived nearby, organized itself to meet a new crisis.

Darkness fell as the ambulance sped toward the hospital in Hyannis. The driver's eleven-year-old nephew, who was down from Vermont for a visit to the Cape and had come along for the ride, was given the responsibility of operating the flashing red light on the roof. "Maybe someday, when you're older," his uncle told him, "you can be a rescue squad worker too."

I wondered again whether there would be a moon over Rock Harbor and how long it would be before Gladys could see it again.

As it turned out, she never did come home.

The heart condition stabilized, but other things began to weaken. She was, after all, almost eighty-one, although it was hard for anyone who knew her to believe this. What we had thought would be a two- or three-day hospital stay lengthened into a full week, then two . . . five . . . seven. . . . During all that time, the neighborhood support-system never faltered.

Family members, too far away to help full-time, came when they could on weekends. On one occasion, Barbara, David, and I—the original "Stillmeadow children"—together with David's wife, Anne, held a family reunion at Gladys's bedside. The reminiscing was so filled with laughter that a frowning nurse came to check.

"I thought you were having a party," she said.

David, himself a doctor, was not intimidated.

"We are," he said calmly.

But it was the neighbors and friends who provided the day-in, day-out encouragement and attention. They set up a schedule for visiting, so that somebody came every afternoon and every evening. During times when regular visitors were barred, our friend Slim, pharmacist at the hospital, dropped by to say hello.

Every day brought a small gift: a delicate homemade custard, perhaps, or a snapshot of Mill Pond at sunset, a pot of ruffled pink African violets, a unicorn postcard.

Amber too received regular visitors, morning and evening, as neighbors provided her with fresh-cooked tidbits, a leisurely brushing, some reassuring conversation. She ate very little and spent most of her time sleeping but did not seem to be unduly anxious. Meanwhile, Still Cove itself was kept in shining order, the houseplants watered at their accustomed times, the wildlife dinners set out as always.

But the loving support went both ways, for if other people sustained Gladys, she sustained them.

How was she feeling? Better, always better.

How were things going? Very well—everyone was so kind—except that of course she was longing to go home.

The doctor thought perhaps next Monday.

How was the food? Delicious. (This said as an untouched lunch tray was being carried away.) But enough about hospital life. What was the news from home? Was Amber eating well? Were there any new birds on Mill Pond? Any signs of spring in the border? What had the visitor been doing lately? How was the new Irish setter puppy at Holly Hill?

Within the hospital, Gladys quickly formed relationships as warm as those she had in the outside world.

"This is my favorite nurse," she would say, beaming, while the slender young girl in white (surely too young to be a nurse?) smiled back affectionately. "She's getting married next week. This is the very kind gentleman who helps with the meal trays. And I do hope the doctor comes while you're still here. He's such an interesting man—went to Amherst, his wife went to Vassar. They have two teenage children. . . ."

And always, whenever she had even a scrap of extra energy, she would reach for the yellow pad and the felt-tipped pen on the bedside table. "What day is today? There's a column due on Wednesday."

For in the end, this is what sustained Gladys most: her work. No matter what else happened, the weekly column for the local paper, the *Cape Cod Oracle,* must be finished. Once Olive suggested that editor John Hughes would certainly not mind if she skipped a few weeks. After all, most columnists take a vacation now and then. Gladys was shocked at the very thought.

Ideas for book reviews, articles, stories, and especially poems must be written down for future use. (When we cleaned out her desk, we found a whole notebook filled with poems. Nobody had known about it. We felt as if she had left behind a special letter for us. One poem spoke of her own death and we used it in her memorial service; someday all of them will undoubtedly see print.)

Nothing, absolutely nothing—not even what we all came to recognize as a final illness—could shake a commitment to writing that was, quite literally, lifelong.

So the weeks stretched out. The last fringe of ice melted from the rim of the beach. Buds began to swell on the bushes. Before long, the first green tips of the daffodils would poke up. . . .

It was one of those nights when I had stayed over at Still Cove instead of driving back to the city. A March wind was sweeping across Mill Pond and I was lying awake, long after midnight, listening to the sound of the waves. When the telephone rang, I knew even before I answered what the message would be. She was gone.

Amber, who had been curled up, as always, on Gladys's pillow, poked an inquiring face around the doorway. Why was the phone ringing so late at night?

I gathered her up, an armful of satin-smooth fur. "Go back to sleep, little one," I told her. "Everything is all right."

The next morning, the wind turned colder and the weather report warned of snow. Winter was making one last appearance before giving way to spring.

Two days later, the family assembled at Stillmeadow in an Arctic countryside. The drifts were knee-deep along the picket fence, the lilac branches lacy with icicles. Peering out through the haze of falling flakes, we worried about the car and the van that were coming down from Massachusetts in the blizzard. My husband piled extra logs at the edge of the hearth.

At midday, however, the snow tapered off, and by the time we gathered at the little country cemetery, the sun had come out. Someone had shoveled a neat path up the slope to the family plot, and the hemlock trees sparkled beside the open grave. Now and then a branch shifted slightly, letting fall a mist of white. But the casket was springlike with a graceful spray of pink roses, the creation of Gladys's favorite

Cape Cod florist, resting on its softly gleaming blue top.

The service was brief. Our Congregational minister led the prayers and read from Scripture the age-old, comforting words: "O grave, where is thy victory? O death, where is thy sting?" Then Gladys's old friend Joe Tomey, newly ordained as a Roman Catholic deacon, talked about her life and what it had meant to those who knew her in person and to those who knew her through her writing.

Afterward, we went back to Stillmeadow for bowls of soup, hot cheese bread, and homemade cake. On the table, blue candles burned in the milk-glass candlesticks on either side of the spring flowers sent by Gladys's editor, Peg Cameron.

The group was small—only the family members and those few old friends who were almost family—and it fitted comfortably about the fieldstone hearth. We traded memories of Gladys and also of Jill, who preceded her to that same quiet hillside—could it have been twenty years ago? And we recalled the dogs and cats, the friends and family, who had been part of the circle in years past.

It was the sort of occasion Gladys would have loved—good food, good talk, and an applewood fire.

I don't remember who first brought up the idea many of us already had in mind, but someone said, "You know, the burial service was exactly right! Still, maybe we should have some sort of memorial service too. So many people would like to pay tribute to Gladys."

"How about a service on the Cape? There must be a meeting hall in Orleans that we could use." Barbara, the practical one, already had her notebook out.

"When would we have it?" asked David, going to the kitchen for the wall calendar.

"Why not on her birthday, April twelfth?" I suggested, looking over Dave's shoulder. "It comes on a Saturday this year—couldn't be better."

And so it was decided.

With Olive as coordinator, the plans quickly got under way. The old Meeting House that belonged to the Orleans Historical Society would be the perfect location. It was not usually available for public gatherings but the trustees made an exception in this special case. The white clapboard building has tall clear windows and an elegantly curving balcony. A low platform runs across the front of the assembly hall; on it is an old fashioned pump organ. At the back of the hall there is enough space to set up a long table, a very important feature, since the kind of informal gathering we had in mind called for refreshments.

Before long, all the various responsibilities were parceled out. Everybody who wanted to have a share in the service was able to take part in one way or another.

The list of volunteers and their tasks included many of the names that have appeared and reappeared in Gladys's books:

Eileen, decoration of hall (fresh-cut evergreen boughs and, instead of cut flowers, potted spring bulbs in bloom—to be taken home later to people's gardens); Gail, assistant to Eileen and general stage manager; Jimmy, photography before and after service; Helen and Vicky, refreshment table (white wine, cheese, chilled apple juice, coffee, cookies); Martha, cookies; Bobby G., traffic director and usher; Millie, in charge of guest book (must have blue cover); Kay and Pret, white azalea and nut cake; Ed, miscellaneous odd jobs; Davy W., tape recording of service; Rob and Bebe, chauffeur people needing lift; Linda, sitter for Amber; Nancy, get Still Cove ready for family; Barbara and Slim, available all weekend as needed.

In one corner, a pencil sketch of an open menu carried the reminder:

For family supper after service—

Orleans Deli promises TWO trays sliced turkey,
r. beef, ham, etc.

Olive—crock of baked beans
Jan—"special salad"

Finally, listed across the top were the names of people taking part in the service itself, together with their particular themes:

We remember Gladys

—as writer: Hugh Johnson, VP, Lippincott
              John Hughes, editor, *Cape Cod Oracle*
—as friend: Helen Elliot
          Jan Krusen
—as family member: Anne (my daughter)
                    Ellen (Jill's granddaughter)

Prayers and religious meditation: Joe Tomey

Music: Organ, Maggie Ribb (formerly Dr. Bill's assistant,
              now full-time musician)
       Violin-viola duet, Alice and Anne
       Violin solo, Alice

I did not make a list of people who were planning to come, but if I had, it would have been a compendium of people Gladys had known and loved and written about. Erwin and Cathy were flying in from Colorado, bringing the babies. The Lovdals were driving up from Southbury, and so were the Phillipses. A few old friends could not make the long trip—George Bennett, Alice Blinn, the Stephensons, Erma and Joe Vanek, Glenn Richardson (still at sea)—but most of her close friends and many longtime readers would be on hand. In addition, the entire town of Orleans, it seemed, planned to attend.

The service was all we had hoped it would be. The spirit was caught so perfectly in the editorial John Hughes wrote about it that we made copies to send to everyone who had missed the occasion itself.

Cape Cod Oracle, April 17, 1980

Life with Gladys Taber

By John Hughes

The small town of Orleans paid tribute this weekend to a lady with a large reputation.

In the Meeting House of the Orleans Historical Society, aflame with flowers, awash with Bach, relatives and friends paid respect to Gladys Taber on Saturday—on what would have been her 81st birthday. She died March 11.

Although those present had lost a good friend, it was not a mournful memorial service, for it focused on the love and the laughter Gladys Taber brought to life in person and through her writings. In that sense, it was uplifting, as Gladys Taber herself was to so many thousands.

Joe Tomey, a supermarket owner and lay clergyman, gave the invocation and talked about the way Gladys Taber saw beauty in simple things. Hugh Johnson, former vice president at Lippincott, reminisced about Gladys as a writer, occasionally stubborn about grammar and structure, as is the wont of writers.

Some of her close friends spoke and revealed delightful nuggets; for example, how Gladys Taber as an undergraduate at Wellesley had memorized the romantic works of Shakespeare and could trade Keats, line for line, with any expert.

There was mention of her unique filing system. Miss Rogers' flower shop, for example, might be found under "B" or "W" for the name of its owner, Bill Wildman, or "F" for flowers, or "M" for Miss Rogers, the original owner.

Then there were those jolly dinners at the Lobster Claw—and beware the thoughtless guest or granddaughter who ate all the swordfish without remembering to take some home for Amber, the cat.

Her granddaughters played her favorite Bach, and Jimmy De-
Lory, who'd looked after her cars since the 1940's, was there, and
Russ Crosby, who'd looked after her garden, and Howard Sinclair,
the Orleans postmaster who'd handled all that mail from thousands
of fans all over the country.

And everybody shed a few tears, but often of laughter, as a
niece recited her stories about such delectable moments as the time
the favorite dog ate the brand new hat of the special guest.

It was the kind of gathering that strove to obey her 1976 poetic
injunction:

> When I am gone
> I beg no fanfare;
> Indeed I shall not be there
> So no tears need be shed.
> They will not bring to me
> Rock Harbor sunset
> On a burning sea
> Or Amber's purr-song, nor yet
> Wild geese waking me at dawn
> For I shall be dead—
> Then greet the new day
> Pretending I am not away.

And so we supported each other, aware as Joe Tomey said, that
Gladys Taber was beyond pain. And, some of us suspected, off
on a new experience with writer's appetite for detail whetted, and
colorful phrase already being turned.

The weekend came to a close, and people went back to
their work, their schools, their everyday lives. I was alone
at Still Cove. Especially alone because now there was no soft
purr to keep me company: Amber had just faded away, as
if she sensed somehow that this time Gladys was not coming
home from the hospital. She did not even last until the memorial service. I consoled myself by remembering that, before
long, she would be where she most wanted to be: next to
Gladys.

I wandered aimlessly about the house. There was plenty to do. The desk was piled with letters needing to be answered with thanks and reassurances that Still Cove and Stillmeadow would stay safely in the family. Many of the letters came from readers who wrote: "Even though I never met your mother in person, I felt as if she were a dear friend, a member of my own family." And many of them also said, "I can't tell you how much she helped me!"

One message announced that the fifth-grade class of the Orleans Middle School, which Gladys had often visited, had changed the name of its academic team from the Abraham Lincoln Team to the Gladys Taber Team.

There were formal tributes from Wellesley and from Boston University and long, wonderful letters from several of Gladys's high-school classmates: "I will always remember how graceful she was, ice skating on the Fox River."

In addition to the correspondence, there were manila folders filled with notes for her next writing project—all needing my attention. The new book, to be based on her weekly Cape Cod columns, was still set for publication and I had been asked to put it together. Like the columns, it would follow the cycle of a Cape Cod year, starting with April, which she always considered the real beginning of the new year. (January, to her, was simply the midpoint of winter.) The publication date was already set: April 12, Gladys's birthday, a year from now. How delighted she would be, I thought, to know that even though she herself would not be putting the finishing touches to the manuscript, the book was going on as scheduled.

There would be another title to add to her list of publications. The shelves near the desk were filled with Gladys Taber books: her best legacy.

I turned away from the desk. No, I could not settle down to work. The house was too empty—no one reading on the sofa or typing in the wing. And Amber's favorite windowsill, the lookout post from which she kept watch over the front yard in hopes of being able to defend the house from visiting raccoons or opossums, was bare.

I went to the kitchen for a cup of coffee. Glancing out the window I noticed four—no, five—quail industriously rummaging under the rosebushes. It was unusual for them to come at twilight; probably they had stayed away earlier in the day because of all the cars. I found a small pad on the counter and scribbled a memo to myself: "Tomorrow—more bird seed." I had almost forgotten that tomorrow would come.

It was too foggy for a walk, but I had to do something. My mother's solution would have been to reach for a book. It occurred to me suddenly that I should go to one of her own books. In the past, her words had comforted so many people during times of sorrow and pain. Surely, there would be a message for us now.

I found it almost at once.

Gladys herself had often faced the death of someone close to her; she had learned to walk the lonely path of grief. In the end, she had found faith and, with faith, peace. It was in one of her descriptions of this experience that I came across a sentence that spoke directly to us all:

> As for me, I believe we never lose
> those we have loved.

STILL COVE JOURNAL

April

Spring has a fairy-tale quality when it finally comes, misting the earth with green. We talk about it all through the winter months, but when the mystery of growth renews itself, we find it hard to believe. The grass would be miracle enough, but buds begin to swell on the lilacs, delicate leaves lace the trees, crocuses set the table for April with gold and purple cups. Daffodils were a wonder in March simply because they poked their lance tips above the ice at my doorstep. But now they wear proud, ruffled blossoms and everyone who comes stops to greet them.

"How beautiful they are! A lot of mine never came up."

"Well, I lost a lot on the slope. Somebody dug up the bulbs and ate them, I guess. My Blackberry used to love bulbs." My voice is wistful when I speak of my resident skunk, who lived in a burrow down the bank below the split-rail fence. I have written before about him and have told how he vanished when a skunk epidemic swept the Cape. But April always brings him to mind with special vividness, because it was then that he shook off his winter lethargy and began making his regular rounds again. Of course, skunks do not hibernate completely, and I could expect to see him on any fair day in winter. But spring brought him out for good.

Every evening at the same time he huffed his way up the

bank and waddled to the door. If his supper was not ready, he scratched at the sill.

"I'm coming! Be right there!" I would call as I dished up his bowl and carried it out. He led the way to his favorite eating spot by the birdbath. On warm evenings, Amber and I could sit in the yard while he ate. I was surprised that an Abyssinian cat and a big Cape Cod skunk could get along so amiably. If a raccoon turned up after dark, Amber exploded with rage. Murder was her immediate plan.

Blackberry's food was of great interest to guests. "Is that creamed chicken?" somebody would ask. "Chicken fricassee?"

"Only a few leftovers from supper," I would say. "He likes almost anything, so nothing goes to waste."

If we moved slowly and spoke softly, he ignored us. Occasionally he would lift his black satin head and move it back and forth, trying to focus his nearsighted eyes on the closest human being. Then he would quietly return to his meal.

This April, I am told, skunks are coming back, or so it seems. Amber and I keep a lookout at Still Cove. Blackberry's burrow is still there, but his path is long overgrown. I am in hopes that some relative of his may yet turn up and a shy pointed face once again peer out of the bushes at the edge of the yard.

This is the time when all wildlife travels the road to spring. The air is an orchestra of bird music, from the whistling of the cardinals to the sweet lyrics of the song sparrows. The robins are assertive. The sea gulls cry over Mill Pond, a melancholy sound suggesting far spaces of shining sky.

It is an exciting time, especially for those of us who have been intimate with January, February, and March here on the narrow land. Alewives will be running soon: time to fish out the buckets from behind the lawn mower and take off for Herring Run!

All this activity reminds me of something I have often said

before. And since a good idea is worth repeating, I have no qualms about saying it again.

Now in April comes the real beginning of the year. The calendar may insist on putting New Year's in January, but for me April is the true beginning of the yearly cycle. Now everything is new, everything is young.

My personal calendar begins in April too: my birthday comes on April 12. As a child, I sometimes wished I could change the date to sometime in May. There would be less chance then of having a cloudburst on the day of my party. But now I would not trade it for the brightest day in October.

All the bustle of early spring—seedlings uncurling, buds swelling, birds arriving—adds a festive air to my special day. And no one could ask for better gifts than those that April brings: the spring song of a newcomer at the bird feeder or a graceful branch of forsythia just about to bloom. I am sure that something can be said for birthdays that fall at the end of November or in mid-January, but I am glad that mine comes now and that my own new year and nature's coincide. Even the sea gulls seem to be celebrating!

On sunny weekends in April, traffic begins to pour from the mainland. Property owners are easy to detect, for they are already starting to "bring a few things back for summer." Houses and cottages open up like flowers. In recent years we have noticed that more and more people are coming down for weekends all year round, just because they are winter-starved for the rolling surf, the sound of gulls, the infinite horizon of sky, the clear unpolluted air. But at this season, the great bridge is beaded with a string of cars. And we begin to notice that many of them have faraway licenses.

"I saw Idaho at the post office. They can't be here just for a weekend."

"Florida is here too. They must have heat in the house. Or maybe they want to cool off."

The count varies. A recent record gives the population of Orleans as 4,369. But I think they have not counted the brand-new babies I see in Dr. Bill's office! Then the statistic of 30,000 summer visitors probably isn't authentic either. All we know is that there are times when we wonder if it is possible that our beloved Cape will sink like the lost Atlantis.

Meanwhile, spring keeps her customary patterns. The Full Pink Moon rises as usual. Mill Pond is luminescent; the sky is a garden of stars. The smell of spring fills the air. Days may be warm or cold, but Easter is at hand, and the next thing we know, we will be discussing which way to turn our clocks. "Spring forward," we quote. It is a mystery to me why wrestling with my clock will add an hour to my time.

But I am always ready to have spring really spring forward, even if just by one hour! We can look for mayflowers then.

Sometimes I wonder whether we aren't swamped with inventions. I spend a lot of time being thankful for push-button gadgets, electric lights, pressure cookers, and all the rest. Certainly they do make living easy. But today when I was paying bills, I suddenly remembered the days when the milkman came to the back door with bottles—real glass bottles—of fresh milk so rich that the top third was pure cream. His bill was written in pencil on a piece of notebook paper. Mama took it and fished the right amount from the blue teapot on the shelf. Then she tucked the bill into a small tin box with roses painted on the lid. Once a month Papa added up the bills and copied the amount in his big ledger.

Nowadays, the milk comes in a heavy waxed container, and mine often leak. The contents are homogenized, skimmed, pasteurized, enriched with Vitamin D, and so on. This milk has been through a lot since it left the cow. The container has printed instructions: to open, I am to push up a flap. But the flap will not push up. I pinch and pry and squeeze. I take a kitchen knife and wedge the tip in the tightly sealed crack. One flap shears off; the other opens just enough to leak when I try to pour Amber's three tablespoons of milk into her bowl. The battle with the orange juice container is best forgotten because orange juice is sticky.

If I decide on tomato juice, I have to deal with a can. There is a small hole in the cover with a piece of thin metallic sealing tape over it. Yes, it is sealed. When I pull up the tab, a minute rectangle should rise gently. Presumably, the design does away with old-fashioned can openers. Not for me, however. I cannot get a firm enough pinch on that slippery seal to move it. Pincers don't work either. A screwdriver may cope. Or even one of those outmoded can openers.

Cranberry juice and apple juice come in quart bottles with smooth metal caps. Just twist the cap, the directions advise. After wrenching at it until I am red in the face, I bang the top on the sink. Then I run scalding water over it. Then I hunt for a flat circular piece of rubber and twine my fingers around the whole thing. Sometimes this results in my being able to have some juice.

This process goes on with a good many jars: pickles, ripe olives, honey, jams, and conserves. But I now have all such problems solved. I line up the unopened containers on the kitchen counter and wait for the next strong neighbor to drop in. A single twist by a muscular human hand defeats the toughest and most recalcitrant gadget. "Nothing to it," is the brief comment.

Recently, I notice, designers have begun to consider the problem of opening those medicine containers, the plastic bottles with puzzle tops, which are presumably child-proof. They certainly are adult-proof. I advise any adult who has difficulty with them to hunt up a child. Sometimes I myself use a strong nail file to work the arrow around to the right point, whereupon the cap flies off into Amber's interested face and pellets scatter over the floor. But what a heady sense of triumph to manage without a child!

Now we come, reluctantly, to bills. There is a place on the long document that says "Detach here." I am quite willing to comply. First I fold the sheet over and press the dotted line with both thumbs. Then gingerly I begin to detach the top portion. Yes, it detaches all right. It rips off with the lower half of the sheet still attached, hanging suspended. If the tear is minor, I use a French kitchen knife to complete the job; otherwise I get out the scissors and *cut* the rest of the bill in half. I know I must save the bottom section for my records so I keep a roll of Scotch tape handy to patch the tear. (One good invention, along with Elmer's Glue!) The main reason it takes me so long to do the bills is detaching.

I leave to the last those bills that include return envelopes with small plastic windows. Such bills have three parts, not two, and it is important to insert the proper section into your return envelope and be sure that it is right side up, with the correct address showing. My efforts often result in the envelope's being addressed, not to the company that is expecting my payment but rather to a certain Gladys B. Taber in Orleans, Mass. The firm's address was on the top third of the sheet which I have torn off and filed in my desk. I am sure this type of bill saves time for the company, but it certainly wastes a lot of mine.

In short, the life of a modern-age housekeeper may be as easy as falling off a log. But I have never found that so easy. And I could never get the cap off the alcohol bottle so that I could rub my bruises!

Space prohibits my listing all the other small frustrations that plague daily life. Philip Bergson had to fix every inside door at Still Cove recently since none of them would quite close. It is not that I mind open doors as a rule, but when a golden retriever and a poodle come for the weekend, Amber puts all four paws down: some sort of firm barrier is essential. She has to nap in the bedroom, while the poodle presides in the den and the golden takes over the living room. Doors simply cannot stand ajar.

Philip explained what was causing the problem. "The house has settled a bit, that's all. Most houses built on steep slopes do."

But surely this is no reason for the bureau drawers to stick. I have to leave all of mine partly open.

"That's the sea air," Philip says. "Makes those windows stick, too."

I think wistfully of how fortunate Mama was. Papa was not only a geologist but also a resident plumber, carpenter, and electrician. He was always available when something got stuck or broke down. However, only Papa could have almost burned the house down when he absentmindedly added a little gasoline to the coal in the furnace!

The best way to take care of household frustrations, I find, is to shut the door behind you (being careful that it doesn't lock itself) and drive over to Rock Harbor to watch the boats come in. They ride the blue water so proudly as they arrow toward the harbor.

Welcome home, fishermen.

The Canada geese reminded me of a town meeting today when they started arguing in Mill Pond right under my bedroom window. This is their favorite arguing place; their preferred time, unfortunately, is around six in the morning. Amber yawns, stretches, pads across the bed to stare out at the water. She decides that there is nothing to be excited about and folds up again on her pillow. But I begin to think about these magical birds. Sleep is gone for good.

In our town, when the geese go over, neighbors call up or drop in. The long V-shaped flight pattern is beautiful, and it can be seen perfectly from my window. How do the geese

measure it? The haunting sound comes back to earthbound dwellers and echoes some longing in our own hearts. Why is this so? Human beings are not usually migratory.

I myself would not want to take the long perilous journeys the geese take. I am like the few who winter over in the small duck pond at the end of the big inlet. They gamble that Mill Pond will not freeze over, and if all goes well, they are safe in a snug haven all through the winter. This past season, they were unlucky: ice paved Mill Pond almost entirely. One small spot of open water was left near the opposite shore where springs feed a small inflow. To reach it, the geese walked across the ice. All the grace of flight was gone as they flopped awkwardly along. When they finally made it, those of us who were watching felt triumphant.

Now the spring sun shines on the dark blue water, and the sea people have their rich feeding ground again. Sea gulls swoop in circles, buffleheads dive underwater, mergansers drift by. There are so many sea birds dipping and circling that they are hard to identify. I am used to having friends come in the door and dash for the binoculars without stopping to speak to me. For two days a loon perched on a last sliver of ice, flexing his wing muscles and preening, obviously getting ready for courtship. Neighbors came just to see him. Even after he had decided that he was ready and had flown off to some freshwater nesting site, people came just in case he might turn up one more time.

When the sparrow hawk sails by, Still Cove is quiet. This is a bird splashed with bright color and very rare in our area. He almost looks like a tropical bird. My regular, ordinary hawk perches on the tip of a juniper, then dives through the air like a bullet. His flight is imperative and breathtaking. Somehow all the force of nature is in him. I do not believe he is an evil bird: he is hungry and he was designed for the purpose of finding his prey, surviving, mating, and watching his offspring open wide beaks and scream—for *food*. Is he different from the robin stuffing worms into greedy babies?

Mankind is the ultimate predator, after all, and famous for killing his own species. It is easy to imagine what the other species on the planet would say to this strange trait!

Nowadays, though, the main conversation in this neighborhood is planting. (That is, unless a strange bird flies by.) No two gardeners agree on the right time to begin. I go along with the view that the soil temperature must be warm. But eager people have already started indoors, using pots. Certainly transplanting in late May is safe. Then the chilling night winds have gone to wherever winds go to rest.

"Plant by Memorial Day," my friend Linda Toomey advises, uncrossing her long legs so that Amber can jump into her lap. "Then you'll have peas for the Fourth of July."

"Is that an old Cape tradition?" I ask, for Linda is a native Cape Codder.

"I've no idea," she says. "But it works."

For hungry bird-watchers and gardeners who have just come in from "turning up a little" in the garden, I like a dip that goes well with any liquid refreshment. In a double boiler, put one 16-ounce package cream cheese, ¼ cup mayonnaise, 1 tablespoon dry mustard, and a dash of Worcestershire. Mix well as it heats. When it is creamy, add ¼ cup white wine and 8 ounces crabmeat. When warm, serve with toast points, crackers, or chunks of French bread. I use canned crabmeat (drained) unless I have some crab from the Lobster Pool. Jumbo shrimp would be fine too, or how about lobster?

Sometimes even now in April the wind is cutting. We put more logs on the fire as if it were still midwinter. But we know that the first purple blossoms on the lilac will open exactly on schedule.

April is a promise of what's to come.

May

It is possible to type with one finger, although I generally use several. But this morning I had a cat in my lap. Amber was curled up, leaning against my left arm. Her wedge-shaped jaw rested on the bottom of the typewriter. The rest of her five pounds (including tail) needed help to keep from slipping, so my right elbow was involved as a support. My right forefinger was free. I wrote, "This is the month of the Full Flower Moon." Amber's number-three purr—the loudest one—made a pleasant accompaniment. Eventually she went to answer the front door knocker and I followed her.

She does not always insist on helping me type. Just why was she lonely at this time? Her warm sunny pillow on the armchair by the picture window is more comfortable, and the birds, rabbits, stray dogs, and squirrels, are right outside at paw's length. But for some reason, she needed companionship.

Loneliness is a mysterious emotion. I too know that sudden sense of emptiness. The only help is to be very busy at something. If I haven't seen Amber for twenty minutes, I look for her and then give her a good brushing and combing. The feel of her soft, dense fur is a comfort, and her rippling number-two purr is dreamy. These days she is shedding, so we both sneeze as apricot fluff drifts into the air. Her coat is ticked with seal-brown, but the wisps caught in the brush are almost black.

Cat lovers know that every cat is remarkable. I was told of one cat that actually answers the telephone by lifting off the receiver when the bell rings. If the owner is away, the person on the other end of the line could leave a message if only the cat could repeat it later on! Another cat, a long-time Orleans resident, is able to count. She had five kittens and brought in five mice when she hunted. The kittens were laid in a line, then a mouse was laid in front of each one. So—five kittens, five mice. Another cat opens the refrigerator door whenever she is hungry. She swings on the latch. Most cats have a better time sense than humans do. When Jimmy DeLory was a boy, he had a cat that met him daily at the end of the road when he came home from school. The sense of direction is also legendary. Everyone has heard stories of cats who found their way home from incredible distances. Heroism, too, is part of cat lore: cats have warned the family when the house was on fire or saved their kittens from a snake or hawk. (Sometimes these are the very same cats who get stranded in treetops and complain piteously that they are afraid to come down alone. But in a genuine emergency they are cool and decisive.)

Amber is one more remarkable cat. To be sure, she did have the advantage of being taught a few things at a young age, just as my cockers and Irish setters always were. As a result, she comes when she is called—unless a bureau drawer has been shut on her. She comes from the fourth shelf of the bookcase or the bathroom windowsill or from under the electric blanket. She also comes if I have shouted *No, No, No!* when she is clawing the newly upholstered chair. In fact, it is disconcerting to know that whenever I rebuke her, she will fly to my lap for comfort.

Animal-lovers disagree as to how many words a dog has in his or her vocabulary. I have read somewhere that four

hundred seems to be the top level. I once tried to count up all the words that Holly, my Irish, understood but gave up: besides, we did not need words for communication anyway. This is true also with Amber. She seems to think what I am thinking. Whenever I am going out, I always let her know. Halfway through my explanation of how long I expect to be gone, she retires to my bed to wait if I am going out for dinner. If I indicate that I am only making a short trip to town, she sits in the kitchen window to wait. Our communication works both ways: she had no problem telling me she wanted a glass of ice water on the table by the sofa at *all* times.

One thing that cats and dogs both do is listen: unlike many people, they pay attention. And when they bark or miau or growl or hiss, they have something to say. Amber and I have had so many conversations that it took me two books to record them. Holly might have taken three. There is a lesson here, I think, for parents of young children. Small ones who are always told to run away and play are seldom very verbal. Those encouraged to join in the conversation tend to talk early and often. Some philosopher once said that what you invest is the gauge of what you receive. Certainly this is true of animals and children.

And plants! I am happy to see that scientists are now deciding that plants flourish if you talk to them, especially if you praise them. Many gardeners have known this all along. In the early days I myself was considered a bit odd because I talked to my African violets. My family urged me to keep quiet, at least when any visitors were within earshot.

The sky was pale with day's end, but white clouds drifted over Brewster and glowed here and there with pink. They looked like meringues dropped on the blue expanse. My neighbor Olive and I were on our way to see two baby Nubian goats belonging to our friend Russ Crosby. One was three days old, the other only two and a half. We were welcomed by the mother of the older one, along with a gentle springer spaniel, a pompous goose, and four assorted small boys racing toward tomorrow and whooping with the joy of it.

The mother of the younger baby had rejected her so obviously that Russ had been forced to substitute. Now he had to walk softly not to step on this tiny creature. Most of the time he carried her in his arms, so it was easy for me to reach over and gather her up. She was not much more than a handful as she snuggled comfortably against my neck. A miniature tongue kissed my cheek. Pencil legs poked satiny hooves against my arm. Two onyx eyes looked at me wistfully. Who was I? Could I possibly be connected with milk? Why did I cuddle and rub her so comfortably when that other creature just shoved her away?

"Maybe your mother will change her mind," I told her. "I wonder why you have such long, floppy ears?"

It seemed impossible to leave, but shadows were falling through the pines, so I put the baby goat down, noticing how dark her coat was: shadow-dark.

"Her mother may take her back," Russ said once more. He gave us each a dozen big fresh eggs to take home and escorted us to the car. A small shadowy figure stumbled after him, uttering a sound that was half squeak, half wail. When Russ swooped her up, the sound bubbled into silence.

"How did Nubian goats come to our country?" I asked as we drove away. "And where is the Nubian desert anyway? Things jump around so on the map these days!"

We decided to ask Russ the next time we see him.

"What a wonderful afternoon." I said.

"I don't suppose—" Olive said slowly. "No, I don't think I could. . . ."

"Could what?"

"Could make room for another fence in my back yard." She sighed. "With a fence for the garden and the fence for the animals—no, it's not a big enough piece of land."

Fantasy took over. If she had a baby goat—or, better still, two of them—she could get a little cart like the ones in English novels. Then her two cats could ride in it. That would make an impression on Mill Pond Road!

"Especially when one of the cats decided to ride the bigger goat."

Well, it was a nice picture anyway.

As our world becomes more and more mechanized, our closeness to animals is being lost. Big-city zoos bring cows in from the country so that children can see what they look like. And I remember that when my grandchildren, Alice and Anne, were small, their parents searched all over the countryside to find a pig to show them. Nursery rhymes and folk tales were full of pigs, but local farms had not a one. They finally thought of going to the county fair in Connecticut and found a whole tentful of them.

Perhaps the pendulum will swing, and cows, horses, geese, hens, goats, sheep—and pigs—may be part of our environment again. There is certainly a growing interest in just that— growing. Orleans has encouraged a community project similar to those in many areas where people are willing to help the national economy by raising fruits and vegetables. It is a marvelous venture, but it does have problems. There must be available land and water. Poor soil needs fertilizer, lime, peat moss, and the old standby, manure. Gardening takes a lot of time and effort.

What happens in many towns is that these community planting areas become a focus of controversy. At first, eager gardeners get their allotments, invest money and work, and everything flourishes. But then, all too often, the situation changes. The water rate goes up in the town or its original donor moves to the Virgin Islands. Three of the committee members are now involved in businesses which do not supply plows or harrows. Topping it all off, it may turn out that the land cannot be leased again because the Shining Seas Development Company bought it in January. And so the dream project dies.

Nevertheless, in many places, the work does go on. And it is amazing how a worthwhile cause draws people together. Somehow, in spite of all the problems, the community plots get planted and crops grow. And a good many people drawn together by the crisis form lasting friendships (although some feuds, like weeds, grow too).

It is pleasant to think that every community might eventually have a garden area. It would be especially important for people who have no adequate space of their own. Meanwhile I notice that a good many family gardens are thriving these days in back yards, side yards, and even on front lawns.

Here at Still Cove this season, Martha and Olive have been planting for me. Instead of looking out at a mowed lawn by the wing, I will be seeing tomatoes ripening, peppers greening, and maybe a few of those peas that outdo the edible-podded kind. Now you eat the pods and never mind the contents!

It won't be long. Meanwhile, keep the birdbaths full.

The season for class reunions is beginning now. Several of my friends never miss one, adding the years triumphantly. Others say they wouldn't be caught dead at a reunion. (I point out that nobody could be caught dead anywhere.) I myself went to one college reunion for an odd reason. I had never been invited to join the Shakespeare Club, although Shakespeare was my idol. After four years of waiting, I got it through my head that I was not the type to be chosen for such an elite circle. I was about as inconspicuous as one pea in a pod. My life was not blighted by the rejection, but I remembered it when, years later, I was invited to a reunion as a guest of the college.

So I bought some new clothes and some uncomfortable high-heeled shoes. I had an elegant hair-do which made my head itch. And off I went. I knew I had made a mistake as soon as I saw the towers of my Alma Mater. I began to cry in the taxi, and I cried whenever I could sneak into a secluded spot during the whole celebration. It was quite simple. I cried for the past. I didn't want to be all dressed up and chatting over chicken salad with the other alumnae. Only a couple of those who had been closest to me were at the reunion, and I had trouble remembering the names of their children. I did hear about the mishaps, illnesses, and tragedies of everyone.

What I wanted was to be running along the shore of the lake with my two best friends. (Both of them could run faster.) With wind-blown tangled hair, rumpled gym shirts, and faded shorts, we may not have resembled the Three Graces, but we were happy. My head was full of dreams—the rose-covered cottage at the end of the lane being the most important. I had a letter in my pocket that very day promising it.

So at reunion time, I do go back but not to the impressive modern campus of today. Nowadays my very own dormitory has extra wings on it. Certainly my teddy bear is not in room 234, and a Hollywood poster may be on the wall over my desk where the picture of Keats used to hang. But I can look out at Mill Pond and imagine it is the campus lake: on the shore a canoe is waiting so that my roommate and I can drift toward a perfect tomorrow.

Besides, I have a private reunion of my own that is not like any other. Mine is in mid-May and depends somewhat on the weather. It is always a moonlit night, however, for it is then that my unicorn comes. There are many legends about the unicorn, and I began reading about him when I was very young. One I liked most was that the unicorn did not get on Noah's ark because he came by himself, not obeying the two-by-two rule. Another version was that the unicorn galloped up just as the ark cast off. Either story explains the shortage of unicorns from then on.

When I lived in New York City, I often visited the Cloisters to see the unicorn tapestries. The unicorn himself is symbolic of more than can be expressed, but in many of the legends he is associated with the purity of the virgin, who is the one creature able to approach him. The horn of the unicorn has magical power and protects against poison and illness. Our bookstore, the Compass Rose, gave me one of the most beautiful books about this magical creature, *The Unicorn Tapestries,* by Margaret B. Freeman,* which I keep by the sofa.

But my own personal unicorn just happened to come out of the old apple orchard on the hillside above the pond at Stillmeadow, our farm in Connecticut. It was a time of tragedy for me, and I had gone down to the pond to be alone. Moonlight rippled in the grass, which was starred with wild violets. The pond had one splash of silver on the dark surface. The air smelled of flowers and cool water. And there came my unicorn, his delicate silver hooves hardly crushing the violets. At the edge of the pond, he dipped his silver horn and lipped the sweet water. Then he looked at me, his dark gaze steady with wisdom. I did not move. Our silent communication lasted a minute or two; then he turned and moved up the hill, scattering apple blossoms as he went.

I began writing about him almost at once. Friends accepted him mostly as another one of my notions. But lately unicorns have become popular. They appear everywhere: in figurines, lockets, bracelets, crewel work, paintings, chinaware. Still Cove is furnished with them: the small crystal ones on the windowsill look out on the pines and still water. I don't really expect everyone to believe in my legendary friend, but I was happy when one woman wrote me that although her

* Published by the Metropolitan Museum of Art, New York.

husband had no patience with fantasy, when he read a piece I had written, he said, "Well, if she says she saw a unicorn, she did. That's all there is to it."

Actually, we all need some magic in our lives. If life is too pedestrian, it is a bit flat. Especially in this mechanical age, a side trip to fairyland is good for children—and for adults too!

May itself in Cape Cod is magic. It is a flowering time and a time when the air is full of birds. I even have purple finches, which are rare this near the sea. The gulls swoop endlessly over Mill Pond. I like the sharp wild cry—it seems to be wistful, lonely, yet somehow triumphant. In a way it is the voice of the sea herself. Now even the surf is as significant as the cry of the sea gulls.

As I start to wash the breakfast dishes, I sing my own off-key song: "Oh, beautiful Cape Cod—beautiful Cape Cod."

The sky was restless with clouds this morning when Amber began pawing at me to wake up. It wasn't breakfast time as yet, and I don't know what roused her or what made her think that she should rouse me. But somehow the clouds intensified the blue of sky and water, so I did not mind getting up a half hour early. It was worth it: a pure wash of polished pearl painted the horizon above the great beach. I did criticize Amber a bit for upsetting the time schedule, but I had the experience of watching a new world. It may be there are places on the planet that have a sameness, but on this slender stretch of land penciling into the ocean, no day is ever the same, no hour even. This is one reason why nobody ever needs to be idle here. Just watching sky, sea, and land is a complete occupation.

"I suppose you sit here all day and look at your wonderful view," a visiting stranger says. "Of course, at home in Missouri, I have to work."

I say nothing. At this point Still Cove is as usual. The

washing machine (which is stationed in the hall outside the living room) is going with the usual subdued thunder. Nancy Colbert, the neighbor and friend who helps keep the establishment in order, is cleaning the garage floor since the raccoons carpeted it with trash in the night. Philip Bergson is hammering away in the bedroom, making some repairs. Amber is skating on a pile of mail on the sea chest, which will only cause me an extra hour of sorting.

Naturally the telephone rings, and someone who is using an old recipe of mine cannot find how long to cook Indian Pudding and did I really mean to pour a cup of *cold* milk over it before baking?

Eventually there is a lull at this quiet little house by the sea. But then two campers grind into the driveway. The travelers want to know how to get around Mill Pond. And where is the road to Nauset? Not here: they have to go back and start again on the other side. I admit that it is difficult in our town to get to where you aim to go unless you already know the way. So many signs point in the wrong direction or are bent backwards. North and South are confused too, but only Cape Codders know this and it's no problem for us. We tell directions by checking the sun and moon, and time by watching the tides. You cannot expect strangers from Oskaloosa to understand.

Anyway, there comes a moment when I look out of the picture window and feel complete satisfaction. I could pick up handfuls of unadulterated beauty. I do not, however, have time to relax into daydreams, because at that moment Nancy pops in, her charming face bright with excitement.

"Have you looked out of the window?"

"Well, I was just watching some gulls."

"Look over there. A boat just tipped over!" Nancy points to the far side of Mill Pond. "Three men in it. Tipped right over."

"Can they swim?" I have a flair for unanswerable questions.

"Who knows? They seem to be hanging onto the boat. It is *flat* upside down."

Nancy has the field glasses out. I myself have never been able to focus them; I always see double. But I can see the men, all right, and also a second rowboat oaring rapidly toward them.

"If they don't get pulled in right away," I say, "we'd better call the police. People who go fishing in small boats can seldom swim."

"He's hauling one on a rope," Nancy reports.

The next half hour is busy. All three do get safely into the rowboat. One even swims a few strokes while waiting his turn. Their gear is obviously lost in deep water. A jeep turns up at the town landing, and the rescued fishermen drip off home.

There might have been a drowning but there was not. Today there was a nearby boat to help—how often in life is help nearby in time of trouble? I had time to recall quite a few cases in my own life before the rescuer finally dragged one floating oar to his boat.

The postscript to this incident was that the fishermen came back after hot showers and dry clothes and fished another hour. They had a fine haul too, according to one of their wives.

As the afternoon light begins to fail gently, my electric timer bangs the living room clock into lighting the room. Amber decides that she is ready for some of the flounder left over from last night. Nancy has to rush across to Rock Harbor to feed the two senior-citizen Airedales she is dogsitting with.

Mill Pond is quiet again. One small, lone turquoise boat is moored in the middle. There are three—maybe four—people in it, one standing up. (Obviously they have not heard about the previous accident!) They must be catching a good batch of flounder, for they stay in the same spot. Only when

the delicate fingers of dusk slide in from the wooded shores
will they pull anchor and start for the town landing.

So at last I have a little time to view my beloved Mill
Pond. This was not a day for dreaming, but a day that goes
like sand in an hourglass.

With Memorial Day, the Cape begins to realize that the
summer people are here—some for a weekend, some for
the whole vacation. We never know which Memorial Day
is the real one, but two trips to the cemetery would take
care of both. The parade date is announced by our local
radio station in Bog Hollow. There is always something moving about a parade, but this one has added significance in
times of world unrest. Too many wars have destroyed too
many of the young and brave. Too many families in devastated
lands have been left homeless and hopeless. But when the
apple trees bloom on sunny hillsides and lilacs lean against
attic windows in old farmhouses, it is easy to have faith that
peace will someday endure among all nations.

And here on the narrow land, the air is full of birdsong
and summer is just around the corner!

June

June is to me a month of serenity. The weather is as stable as it ever can be on Cape Cod. The first springtime growth settles down into the regular seasonal maturing. Pruning time is over; lawn mowers swing into action. The smell of new-mown grass is lovelier than attar of roses. At noon the beach people spend more time sunning than swimming. And although it is the month of the Full Hot Moon, nights are cool as a mountain brook, the air is sweet.

It is time to think about putting out the houseplants. I get the feeling they have worked all winter to cheer us up and now would like a chance to get away from it all in the real peace of nature. Certainly my poinsettia deserves a vacation. She is five years old and has led a rugged life. She was left out too long one year and was glassy with ice when we rescued her. Another summer, because of family illness, she was ignored for a while and a drought blistered the long, pointed leaves. Once a sudden gale toppled her so she almost drowned in a mud puddle. Even being in the house is no insurance, for the electricity went off during the classic February storm, and the furnace of course went with it. Amber and I made out with cashmere shawls, but wrapping a leggy, tall poinsettia would not work out at all.

"This poor thing has had it," said my friend Millie Connors

at last. "Time to go to the dump. I'll take it on my next trip."

I knew she was right as she invariably is. It was purely accidental that the limp skeleton was still on the dough chest in the wing when I discovered one leaf on a lifeless stem. So was it lifeless after all? I put off the trip to the dump. The plant looked like the aftermath of a tornado, but that one leaf was a bit larger the next time I watered the robust African violets, so I gave the bony skeleton a good drink and some words of encouragement.

Now guests who drop in ask, "What is that? What kind of plant? It isn't—no, it couldn't be."

"Yes, it is—it's a poinsettia."

The brave survivor is about three feet tall. Green foliage cloaks the gaunt stalks (they are all a bit twisted). At the end of every branch, the leaves turn pink. They do not exactly make a poinsettia blossom like an open scarlet fan; they turn pink wherever it is easiest. Some keep the original lime green at the tip.

This odd-looking plant towers over the violets and azaleas on the chest. Frankly, I love it. When crises arise, as is the habit of crises, I go and check my poinsettia, the evidence of five years' battle against seemingly hopeless odds. Should a plant have better courage than a member of what we call a superior species?

This summer the veteran will go outdoors again, but to a corner of the protected terrace (Cape Codders call it a "farmer's porch"), where the sun will not burn it. The pot is too heavy to lift easily, but if we get a bad storm, I am determined that somehow we will lug it inside. I shall not worry about cutting back until some fall day when Millie gets out the pruning shears and says, "Nothing to lose. Let's go."

Everything flourishes in June, of course. Perhaps of all the wild fruits the strawberry is my favorite. The wild berries do not look much like the tame ones (which do look tame in their neat, cultivated rows). Wild strawberries are tiny, fingertip-size, and are scattered like gems at the edge of the meadows. It is well worth a lame back to fill a basket with them. I agree with my granddaughters that the plump, glossy wild blackberries are easier to pick and the baskets fill much faster. But in early summer, when the girls are not on the beach, they are hunting strawberries.

The Cape soil is comfortable with garden strawberries, and great beds of them prosper at its upper end. Growing the giant juicy royal scarlets is an industry, and just to drive by the fields gives a sense of wonder. No one could call this a barren land! A friend of mine once transplanted twelve wild strawberry plants and for three years picked a quart of spicy ripe berries from the green citadels of the plants. Then mysteriously the crop ran out. Perhaps three years was their life span. Or perhaps some unusual condition of nature hurried their departure. It is possible that being cultivated was too much for them. I have noticed that trees often seem to do well just after transplanting but then begin to wither in a short time. I have never been a good transplant myself. Where my roots are comfortable, I thrive best.

Traditionally, June is wedding month, and this year we will be celebrating one in our family. The bride is Jill's granddaughter, the groom a fellow graduate of Yale Law School. They will pursue their careers after the wedding. Mark is a handsome, steady young man, with a clear gaze and no beard to hide his firm chin. Ellen has the fresh loveliness of a new-blown rose. She is exuberant, vibrant, and sunny enough to face life with no fears.

They will be married in church.

"We'll have a forty-eight-hour honeymoon," Ellen says happily. "And then we start our jobs."

Their happiness makes me wonder why so many young couples today distrust marriage. They are willing to undertake the adventure of living together but do not want to make a real commitment. So they hesitate to give their relationship any legal status.

I for one have faith in the old traditions. And I do not believe that the family is doomed. I think it is natural in our society to have close-knit units, a firm basis for successful living. So as June steps softly across the blossoming land again, I hope there will be many weddings to celebrate and that all of them will be blessed with old-fashioned peace and joy.

The arrival of the first peas is the real signature of summer. The gardens brim with those delicate snippets of green, and the contest as to whose peas will ripen first is over, with almost everybody coming out even! Gourmet gardeners pick while the pods are still slim, before (as one of my neighbors puts it) the pods need to join a weight-watchers' class. And oh, the flavor! The new variety, sugar peas, which are eaten pod and all, don't surprise me, because I have been eating pods for years, even before we planted the Edible Podded or Chinese peas. When shelling fresh-picked peas, it is always good to nibble on a few pods. And you may find yourself consuming so many of the green pearls that another trip to the garden is inevitable.

Too many vegetables ripen at about the same time, but a good cook can "work them in," as Mama used to say. The first tassels of the early corn are appearing now. Sweet corn should of course be picked while the kettle is boiling, rushed into the water, and then fished out before it has time to think. Plates should be hot, butter melted, seasoned salt and pepper at hand, and plenty of paper napkins stacked by each plate. According to a Cairn puppy I know, the paper napkins are also edible and they *do not* upset his sturdy stomach, but the rest of us settle for the golden, juicy kernels, smelling of summer.

In our early years of gardening, we experimented with all the possible varieties of corn, including the long, pointed, ivory Evergreen, the mottled Mexican, a pale blue corn, and the regular golden types that photograph so well in the catalogs. We never found one we weren't addicted to after one bite, dripping with butter.

So gather ye rosebuds while ye may, but don't forget to hoe the vegetables!

"I have to tell you something," said Maggie.

It was a day like a dream suddenly turned into reality. Outside the doctor's office, lilacs were blooming and birds sang their June songs. Inside, two small boys delved into the toy chest for more tiny plastic cars to throw around while they waited for Mama to come from the inner room with the newest baby, who would be beaming and waving a sticky lollipop. (How would the world turn without lollipops?) Sunlight was bright as it poured into the waiting room, erasing the memory of icy winter days. The big aquarium on the window ledge had no fish; they were retired long ago in favor of the exquisite miniature lead figures the doctor creates in his cellar workshop. On this day, as always, I was caught in the magic of a scene with a regiment of marching men, each smaller than my little finger. They were stepping along proudly and why not? They were all soldiers who had lost one arm in battle. But this one-armed regiment was ready to give the other arm to Queen and country if necessary.

"So what is the news, Maggie?" I finally waded through toys to her desk.

"I'm leaving," she said.

"Maggie! You can't be!"

"I know. I feel the same way. But it seems to be time. My husband says—excuse me." Maggie picked up the phone and listened to the symptoms of a caller.

Maggie does not look like a medical secretary (although, come to think of it, I am not certain just how one should look). She is small, delicate, and soft-voiced. Fine dark hair frames a wistful face. I am sure that somewhere in a Renaissance painting is Maggie's portrait, the white-robed saint or haloed Virgin standing in a shadowy wood with a few wild animals lying quietly at her feet. The small wild creatures in the office often do curl up near her when she tells them in her gentle way not to tear the toy engines apart.

I finally got the facts. Maggie has a major gift for music. She is church organist, director, and composer. There had to come a time when such a God-given gift became a demand. The arrival of a wonderful new organ for a church in Eastham may have emphasized the point. In any case, she had agreed to play it for an inaugural concert. And one cannot practice while advising patients to put on cold compresses until the doctor can be consulted.

Maggie, I know, faces a dilemma that many young women share today. She is happy in her office, working with a doctor she admires, appreciates, feels close to. She must have a sense of satisfaction at her ability to run the intricate machine of a busy M.D.'s office, but even more because she can give the patients courage and comfort, which she offers quietly and with a smile and a blush, as if nobody really should pay attention to her. At the same time, there are her personal needs and special gifts to consider. And her home life is also important.

I realize how fortunate I was, when I was her age, to be able to work at my bedroom desk, typing away right at home while the oven was set at 350 degrees and the end of a story signaled time to take the chicken out. Today, countless young wives have to decide between that eight-hour day at the office or staying home with the baby, a couple of puppies, a kitten, and a husband who likes meals on time. Even when

husbands and wives share the housework as partners, life
can be exhausting. All too often, it is the budget that is the
deciding factor. Other women must choose between a de-
pendable office paycheck and special studies or a career in
the arts, remuneration uncertain. The choices are never easy.

Now Maggie's path will not cross mine as often. She will
not be sitting at that desk with the red lamp above her. She
and I have been friends for a long time. During a period
when I was shoved in and out of hospitals, she was like a
beacon. Her cheerful encouragement was a constant blessing.
Then when she lost her dog, I suffered with her. I knew
how she felt: hunting all night, coming to the office with
heavy eyelids and trembling hands, answering phone calls
that reported only that the dog was still missing and that
even our efficient police had not been able to find any clues.
Having been through it myself, I remembered so well; and
we had another bond. I will miss seeing her during my regular
visits to the doctor. But I know that her music must have
its turn.

Another special friend is Ruth Hunt, the elementary school
librarian. Not long ago I went to a farewell reception held
in her honor. Children who have been fortunate enough to
know Ruth have discovered the joy of learning. And they
will always feel at home in libraries. I think most of them
could run a library, right now in fourth or fifth grade, whereas
I could not manage a file card system.

The library itself is a very special place. It is full of sunshine,
which floods one whole side of the big room. A couple of
comfortable, gaily colored sofas are there. On the day of
the reception they were filled with non-readers: heroes, hero-
ines, dragons, tigers, all come from the books on the shelves
to live with the children. They are not stuffed toys at all
but evocative personalities. They are delighted to be borrowed by loving children, and they add extra charm to reading. Their creator, Marilyn Whitelaw, has a magic needle

as well as creative skill. I carried the Kipling tiger around with me the whole time I was there. He has soft silken fur, a lithe body, a dark tail meant for lashing, and a sunny face under prick-up ears. I hope he gets borrowed often (and Kipling gets read!).

George Hunt, Ruth's handsome husband, escorted us to the reception, and I was happy to think they could talk over this farewell party in their charming home when the tall doors of the elementary school closed. I hoped there would be enough cookies and cake crumbs for the tiger, the elephant, the little ducks, and all the rest of them.

On the way back to Still Cove, I took time for a series of small errands. Every one of them was also a social visit. And it occurred to me that the people closest to us, those who fill the greater part of our lives, are not the social friends who come for dinner. They are those who help us in the mechanics of living. It is Bob, for instance, who understands the idiosyncrasies of my car; Bev and her two charming helpers at the Lobster Claw who remember exactly how much dressing I like on the crab; and another Bev in the bank who accepts my lack of financial sense with such grace. The list is long. Shopping for groceries at Ellis's Market is especially pleasant because Ruth Wilson is behind the cash register. And at the beauty shop, Janie makes the misery of sitting under the dryer as easy as possible.

When I lived in New York City, I cherished the few friends like the gentle Polish couple who ran the laundry next door. When they showed me the two gold chalices which were all they had left when they escaped from the homeland, my own hardships struggling in a free country seemed like nothing. The Irish grocer across the street managed to save special fruits for me at a reduced price. He too knew what it was to be homesick and short of funds. Every morning he missed the sound of the birds in the thatched roof of his home in Ireland.

But outside of the neighborhood, the city is too big for such friendships. I never had the same saleswoman at Altman's, one who would tell me how dreadful I looked in a yellow dress. Repair men who came to the apartment were seldom the same and never agreed about why the radiators hissed like snakes. But the second time we had to call a plumber in Orleans, Larry Baker said, "Oh, yes, you're the people on Mill Pond. I expect it's the hot water." And as long as he lived, he understood every plumbing problem Still Cove ever had. And took care of them all.

There is an important lesson in this, I think. The way we behave is going to affect the lives of our fellow men even in the most casual contacts. Who wants to be remembered as that woman who snatches the last loaf of Portuguese bread or box of fresh strawberries from the counter? Who likes to be known as that driver who cuts in and gets the last available parking space by the Cape Cod Bank and Trust? Almost all of our actions are interactions, and when we least expect it, we are affecting other people.

So now, as summer begins and the world comes across the bridge and life changes its tempo, may we all be as gentle as June!

On a warm June day it is easy to forget winter. As the mockingbird, song sparrows, blue jays, and mourning doves dip into the birdbath, and Tiny Tim, the red squirrel, takes a flying leap to the roof of the feeder, I wonder whether they remember the snow. I can argue that squirrels store nuts, but do they really think ahead to January or are they like people who fill attics with old *National Geographics* "just in case we might need them some day?" Do the toads dig six inches underground in order to prepare for winter or do they simply burrow down because they feel cold? A neighbor recently spaded up three small toads as he lifted his shovel. What in the world did they think, I wonder? What did it

mean to emerge from the moist, cool darkness of the earth into the bright warm air? Nature is full of unanswered questions.

It is probably pure instinct that settles the nest-building schedules and the time for nestlings to leave home. But there is leeway all the same for individual reaction. I will never forget the day when I watched a father cardinal stuffing tidbits down the throat of an exhausted mama. I was sure he communicated his feelings to her.

"Presently they will all fly away. They won't jam the nest any more, screaming day and night for food, food, food. There isn't room for them in the nest now anyway."

"I told you it ought to be bigger."

"Next year, next year."

"Besides, I've had enough of egg laying. I want some time to be myself. How do I know who I am?"

When their offspring did fly away, I knew what would happen. The nest would be empty, all right, not a single squawk left. But before long two very nervous cardinals would be back, crossing and recrossing the yard, calling and calling. They would want those brawling youngsters right back in the nest. For all of us on this planet have something in common, and emotions about children seem to be shared by many of earth's inhabitants.

Speaking of unanswered questions, there is one that my friends and I cannot solve. The monster road-building machines sleep quietly in their own nests—off the highways— most of the year. But now in June they rouse with roars and growls and heavy puffing. They grind along the roads, dropping orange cones wherever traffic is heaviest. Barricades go up and police arrive to guard the area. All summer, when traffic has no lull, the road repairing goes on full speed. Corners are rounded off (Eldredge Parkway into Route 6), potholes are filled with the usual black soup which solidifies and then swells to make bumps. A few roads are widened. All this work is necessary, and we appreciate it. But cannot it be done at summer's end, just as the tourists and summer residents cross the bridge? Traffic lessens, the weather is usually mild but not hot enough to turn the tar to syrup, the crews would work in reasonable comfort, drivers would suffer only minor inconvenience. Or if it isn't practical to make repairs just before winter sets in (bringing with it the possibility of new damage), then why not do it in May? Roadwork conditions are excellent then.

It is one of the unanswered questions of modern living. But perhaps the schedule is changing after all, for I saw road workers on Tonset yesterday, and the full season is not yet begun.

Roads differ in personality a great deal, I think. Some remind me of sleepy dragons that suddenly stir, which explains those ripples that appear overnight all along the road. One whose name I won't mention is a colicky baby. No matter how often it is repaired—even sometimes out of season—it requires a very steady driver. Otherwise, sudden jerks and bumps will send unwary heads spinning. Mine has gone so far as to hit the windshield. I would recommend that strangers on Cape Cod drive gently until they know our roads.

I have one friend who was away for some time on family business in the wilds of California. The day she got back, she had Jimmy DeLory fill her car with gas. "I hope nothing has changed," she said.

"I think you'll find the same old potholes," Jimmy said.

Later, when she reported the conversation to me, she added, "You know, if the holes on River Road get any deeper, we'll be able to see China."

June, I have recently learned, is the month when the vacuum cleaner was patented. The date was 1869. This morning I took my iced tea out by the bird feeder and sat there for a bit, thinking about housework and cleaning chores. As far as I know, the earliest cleaning aids were brooms and rags held by work-worn hands. One of the first objects I remember noticing when I experimented with walking was Mama's Bissell carpet sweeper. The Hoover vacuum cleaner entered our house much later. I hated it. By then I was old enough to help around the house, and my special chore was to clean the bedrooms. This always involved a battle with the temperamental machine. Even today, I am not exactly on friendly terms with it. Most women I know operate a vacuum cleaner with aplomb, just exactly that. But for me, the vacuum chooses its own route, banging into every chair and table in the room and finally attacking the doorjamb. Why don't I steer it? Well, if the cord did not wind around my ankles and the hose around one knee, I might maneuver better.

The most modern version of this particular cleaning aid is a great success, so I am told. There are outlets built into the house itself, one to a room, and the hose plugs in. The debris finishes in the cellar. I first saw this system when Olive installed it in her house. It would be a blessing, she said, especially for sandy rugs. I remembered suddenly my father's favorite cleaning aid: a fancy wire rugbeater. It was fan-shaped and very heavy and when Father wielded it, the dust flew and sometimes part of the rug threads too. But the carpets did get clean and he had some vigorous exercise.

Woman's Suffrage (in 1919) did more to alter our lifestyle than any other change, but I have a feeling that the advent of the vacuum cleaner was an important step in the emancipation of women. And when waxing equipment was added, women could get up from their hands and knees and stand erect while they kept their homes clean.

Housework can wait on a bright June day, while Amber and I go out to sit in the yard for a while. She tiptoes over the grass, eyes intent, tail lashing, while I turn the old redwood deck chair to a better angle. If I sit musing long enough, my red squirrel, Tiny Tim, comes to the birdbath. The bowl rests on a circle of bricks flat on the grass. Many of the ground-feeder birds were pleased when we moved the bath to floor level, but the rabbits, stray dogs, and especially the squirrel are delighted. He stands on tiptoe so that his chin tops the edge of the bowl. His forepaws brace his delicate body. He drinks rapidly, his feathery tail flicking the air. Cardinals, catbirds, mockingbirds watch him from the rail fence. When he skims away, they swoop down alternately to bathe and drink. Amber ignores them. She is tracking a mouse. But if she were to flick one velvet ear in their direction, everyone would vanish at once, leaving only the sunlight and the breeze moving among the leaves.

This year when the ice on Mill Pond broke up, a new visitor appeared on the fringe nearest shore: a heavy bird, dipping and rising and flapping his wings but not getting airborne. The motion looked like a dance, and some research proved that it was indeed; he was a loon and he was getting ready to go courting. A dashing figure he was, too, silhouetted against the ice, his powerful lance of a beak and pointed jet head tilted against the wind. His body was snow-white ticked with black, the under part all white. Since it was winter, my loon had solid black instead of checkered plumage.

After his graceful ice dance ended, he swam in the open water. Peterson calls him "a submarine-like swimming bird." He soon veered toward the duck pond, which is a country club for Canada geese, mergansers, herons, ducks, and, obviously, loons (if any). That night I heard his cry and could understand why experts have such trouble describing it. At times it is wild and haunting, at times like sardonic laughter. There is hopelessness in it. But to me there is music in it too. It echoes of something greater than our boundaries. Since the loon has lived on this planet 110 million years, there are those echoes. When the experts tell me that the loon is the most primitive bird in North America, I listen with awe although I have never been able to understand how they estimate time. I accept their knowledge and also the report that loons are one of the endangered species. The stories of man's senseless murder of these beautiful birds are sickening. During the rearing season, boats run down the young for sport. Since loons have only two offspring in a clutch, it is easy to reduce the population drastically. The chicks are fragile and spend most of the time riding on the parents. Just why it should be good sport to crash into the wee fluffballs perching happily on Mama's back is a question impossible to answer. We can only pray that after 110 million years, our generation will not record the destruction of the last loon.

Thinking of this makes me proud once more of those Cape Codders who join the campaign to rescue starving wildfowl during the winter. They have saved countless birds that would otherwise have died. Last season, three men came alternately to Still Cove, climbed down the steep icy steps to the wind-scourged beach, trudged to the inlet by the duck pond, and emptied big heavy burlap bags of lifesaving cracked corn. Many birds died all the same, but many more were saved. The men used to stop and tell me how the seabirds fell on that cracked corn. It took a lot of money to buy the feed and many people chipped in; a great deal was donated, and the good men who delivered it to the starving creatures asked no reward.

The last day, the third man climbed the steps up the bluff and I invited him in.

"No, thanks," he said. "I have to get back. But look what I found."

He held up a big, beautiful bird—frozen rigid as marble.

"Poor thing was starved, too," he said.

It was a loon!

"God bless you for trying," I said.

Now in the warm golden days of June, I hope the duck pond has a few fuzzy, bright-eyed baby loons learning to paddle safely.

The English poet George Herbert, writing in the 1600s, spoke of spring as a time "full of sweet days and roses." He could have been thinking of Cape Cod in June—the days are very sweet and roses are blooming everywhere.

July

Just when the exact peak of summer comes is hard to say. The Full Buck Moon of July does seem brighter and rounder, but maybe because the dreamy summer night makes it seem so. On the Cape the gardens blaze with color—and the beaches with sun umbrellas. The tourists, alas, wear fewer and fewer bits of fabric. There never seems to be a gentle medium for Americans. In earlier times, ladies wore long black stockings and bathing suits with sleeves and plump bathing caps. Now they tie a brief string around two parts of their well-oiled anatomies and skip lightly into the water. I am glad that the dreadful old-fashioned bathing costumes have vanished along with the bathhouses that once rolled to the edge of the water, protecting the gentlewoman's privacy. And I do not miss the striped and belted outfits men used to wear. But I do think few human bodies are built like Aphrodite or Apollo: a little cover is a help.

Inland, the hay has a second cutting and silos are being filled. I am sorry there are so few working farms on the Cape. Still, Cape Codders farm the sea, and the crops are rich. With careful management, the harvest will always be good—unless the oil drillers ruin the waters.

Independence Day brings the traditional picnics, festivities, fireworks. The parade down Main Street moves proudly, flags flying. Nowadays we do not hear much of the traditional

Independence Day rhetoric, but our national birthday has not lost its meaning. My favorite definition of independence is Hal Borland's.

"Independence," Hal said once, "means obligations as well as rights. The right to work and the obligation to work at my full capacity." This does not seem to be an age where the word "obligation" is much used, but it is an important one all the same.

There are always special times in midsummer that I tuck away to unpack on dark January nights. One of these came last week when I drove at sunset over to Eileen and Jimmy DeLory's for Sunday-night supper. The road to their house leads through the woods, and that afternoon it looked as if pieces of sunlight had dropped through from the sky. It was so still I could hear the skitter of squirrels in the leaves. The house itself has many happy memories for me. It is low and fits the pine-needled slope that rolls to the clear blue water of the lake. Jimmy has one or two chipmunks who have knotholes in the wide deck facing the lake. If he calls, they pop up and rush to fill themselves with the nuts and tidbits in his hand.

Eileen had set the table by the sliding glass wall so that we could watch the color of the lake change as we feasted on blue crab salad. These are times of anxiety for gasoline station owners and managers such as Jimmy. But he and Eileen face the possibilities with their usual courage.

"Now that Jimmy is closed on Sunday," said Eileen, "I have him home all day. Today we went to Provincetown and took the early morning boatride out to watch the whales— it was wonderful!"

Because of summer, she has cut her hair and it frames her face in soft curls. She wore a brown hostess gown with blue and beige borders from neck to floor. It was as plain as a handkerchief, and the brown silk reminded me of what my mother called China silk, very soft and light.

As the twilight deepened into evening, we did not talk of the bitter state of the world or of the problems ahead; we left that for daytime. We talked about the newest wildflowers Eileen has transplanted into her own woods, and about some interesting books we have read, and, naturally, about children—mine six hours beyond the bridge, theirs in London, Colorado, California. I told Jimmy that a visit like this one was to me like fuel to my car. I pick up speed for the journey ahead.

The elderberry bushes bloom now, lifting clusters of white. When the dark purple berries ripen, it is time to make jelly, and what jelly it is! You do not need to add pectin, the berries provide it. The deep color and spicy flavor make it a very special jelly, just as beach plum is—and both are particularly good with cold meats. To me it seems a waste to invade either of these with gobs of peanut butter!

The fruit stand on Beach Road is ten minutes away and only a block beyond the big white mansion where Janie does my hair. No extra gas to swing past, going or coming. I came in this afternoon still feeling the excitement of Fancy's stand, where the colors of ripe fruit and vegetables are brighter than any painter's palette and the smells are just as beautiful. The stand itself is shaped like a big piano box. You step inside, and the rich spicy perfume of Falmouth strawberries drifts to you. The dark red, plump berries are at their best. I think again of the strawberry fields stretching around that part of the Cape, as prosperous as any Midwestern cropland I know.

But the treasure from Falmouth is not all—nectarines, pastel pink; peaches, now sunset glow; seedless grapes like green ice; new squash, pure gold; onions, pale silk. And tomatoes, smooth scarlet. If the list were complete, it would fill pages, but how to leave out ripe purple plums and bunches of moon-

gold bananas; asparagus spears, dark green; crisp, frilled lettuce; and baby-sized sweet corn and pinky-red potatoes.

Being assailed all at once with the scents, I gave up trying
to describe every separate smell. But they blended like a
tapestry. I did a good deal of sniffing—from the cool fragrance
of green grapes to the heady odor of Bermuda onions.

On the kitchen counter at home, my collection gave new
charm to the room.

The roadside stands are such a familiar part of America
that sometimes we may not take time enough, I think, to
be grateful for them. Now in midsummer, Fancy's has buckets
of annuals on wooden trestles behind the stand. Later on
there will be pumpkins, gourds, corn shocks to choose from.

As I bit into a juicy plum, I thought more about this land
I love. The fruit and vegetable stands are available to any
customer, no ration card required. At our local stand, we
choose for ourselves, then carry the purchase to the sun-
brown, pretty girl who has a gift I envy—she can *add!* Usually
a few other customers are there, so we stop and visit, chiefly
about when it is going to rain—or stop raining. It is comfortable, pleasant, and the whole scene might be painted as "Summer Days, America."

Somehow I think those of us fortunately living on Cape
Cod may be more conscious of our location than many people
in other situations. Like all general conclusions, this is debata-
ble, but I did not do so much analyzing about people and
places when I lived in New York City. Probably it was because
I was always running for the subway.

On the Cape, the normal pace of living is not so much
like a marathon. Last Sunday afternoon, for instance, Olive
dropped in to see about a ride while the weather was so
fine. It would be raining again before long, she said.

A Sunday drive around Orleans rests the spirit. Even when
the turnpike is like one of those domino pushovers, there
are quiet winding roads between the Bayside and Nauset

where the late sunlight rests on fallen pine needles in the woodsy areas. There are gentle old houses with rosy ramblers blooming on picket fences. Anywhere you go there are small ponds of clear water.

"Orleans has such a small-townish look on Sunday afternoon," Olive says. "Children playing, families sitting on lawns, dogs chasing balls."

In the Wisconsin town where I grew up, Sunday was always family day. After church came the big Sunday dinner: chicken with dumplings, fresh vegetables, hot bread, and a light dessert such as fresh peach ice cream (homemade). Then Father, Mother, and I took a ride in the automobile. Father drove at lightning speed, which bounced us around a good deal and scared Mama, but it was a treat nevertheless. We did not swim on Sunday but might go as far as Lake Winnebago, where I could wade a bit.

I feel the same Sunday feeling here on the Cape. Even now in July, there are quiet places. The big beaches may be jammed, but we find the little hidden roads graced with ponds, salt inlets, and leafy woods.

Sunday summer afternoon is a time to cherish.

I think it was Edwin Newman who started the idea of cleaning up our language. I went along with him amiably but without feeling the bones crunch in our civilization. But lately I have begun to suffer what used to be called "nervous fits," which almost always involve expression.

My acute attack began on a dreamy July evening when Amber and I were watching television while sipping iced tea with fresh mint in it. (Amber nibbles a leaf. I munch it.) The program seemed promising: it was an award-giving ceremony for honor students at a couple of educational institutions which I shall never name. I am deeply interested in the future of our young people, and these were endearing because their hair was not long enough to be caught in barrettes, and instead of ragged jeans they wore pants. Several were on football teams, and I love to see my favorite sport allied to academic honors.

The MC gave a fine welcoming speech and turned to the first winner. "How did you happen to choose Environmental Improvement for your project?"

The slim, well-scrubbed teenager blushed, coughed, then spoke in a slightly husky voice. "Well, uh, you know, me and the others felt it would, uh, hm, be an OK kind of thing."

The MC did not flinch. But I nearly knocked my tea glass over.

How could a student get to be an *honor* award winner and not know that *me* is not the subject of any sentence? And hadn't anybody ever said anything to him about the danger of weakening his sentences with all those *hm*'s and hesitation words? All of us make errors, no matter what schooling we have had, and it is very easy to slip into the current jargon. My conversation, for example, acquires a serious uplift when my daughter, Connie, is around. But this was really appalling.

I recovered from my shock on this particular occasion, but worse was to come. A very important person was being interviewed on a talk show. The guest was glamorous and charming. When the MC asked her how she had decided to become an actress, she rippled with laughter.

"It all began when I was in Paris and met J. B. He took my husband and I to dinner—and, well, I got the idea."

If the husband was taken out (as he was later), that sentence was "J. B. took I to dinner." It seemed bad enough that the teenager could have left eighth grade without knowing an elementary fact, but that a VIP had such troubles was extraordinary.

Just as I tried to forget my agitation, an Englishman making a study of what he calls "floppy English" reported that both British and American English are going down the drain. He urged that steps be taken immediately to improve both.

Cleaning up American English is as easy as making a tropical garden out of Alaska, but I think a small beginning might be worth trying. I would make two improvements at once. There is one saying that is thicker than grass blades on a putting green. This is "Of course." "Of course you are familiar with Isham Jones," says the speaker. "Of course you remember what happened after Muhammad Ali's retirement." "Of course you realize it is necessary to let the steam escape from the pressure cooker before you clamp the cover."

Why is "of course" inundating our sentences?

Well, I know a number of fine people who do *not* know anything about Isham Jones. I myself am ignorant of Muhammad Ali's life, as well as his retirement and any subsequent happening. As for the pressure cooker, I do know about clamping the cover since I found out long ago that if you omit this step, the spaghetti sauce hits the ceiling in a great gush.

The "of course" habit is too easy to fall into, partly since it is dinned into our ears by everyone who speaks in public or is on television. It blooms in articles, news editorials, books. I sigh with happiness when Dick Cavett greets his current television guest: his own speech has not lost the echo of Yale. So far I have not heard him assume, ever, that of course his guest, the audience, in fact the whole country knows who first traversed the Nile by kayak.

My second complaint is the repetition of "continue on." This phrase turns up almost everywhere too. The word "continue" is complete in itself; adding the word "on" is unnecessary as well as ungrammatical. If you continue, you are going forward or going on. (I don't object to "he continued on his way" since here the "on" belongs with the phrase.)

Many people have similar dislikes. Connie is crusading against the unnecessary use of "you know" and reports with dismay having found "lay" instead of "lie" in some very dignified prose.

Language is an amazing tool which man developed during the slow rise to civilization. What a mystery it is! Who first made the sound of "Yes"? When did complete sentences come into use? Then I wonder about the differences in countries. Why is the language of every nation different? Scholars can probably explain it, but I can't. And now I have read that ornithologists recently tested various bird species and discovered that birdsongs—or languages—differ in various parts of the country.

Lack of communication between nations has been one of the main causes of war. As air travel brings all people nearer, there will be easier communication and so better understanding. I am reminded of one soldier in a recent war whose life was spared when the rest of his unit fell before an enemy machine gun.

"Why didn't they kill you too?" he was asked.

"I talked to the guy who was about to shoot," he said. "I spoke the same language."

Of course, I could "continue on" about standards of speech, but a certain small Abyssinian cat suggests that it is time for tea.

Thunderstorms come often in July. At Still Cove the view of black tumbling clouds over Mill Pond is magnificent— that is, if you happen to appreciate thunderstorms, which I don't. The vast sky above the Atlantic is split with lightning. During the last big storm I watched five bolts plunge simultaneously into the ocean. These were not single bolts, either, but forked. It looked as if some invisible hand were stitching the sky.

I wonder what the black-winged sea gulls think. Some of them do fly in from the big water to Mill Pond, often coming

early enough to warn us the storm is on the way.

The inland birds vanish into the shelter of the woods, and Tiny Tim takes off with a slice of bread. In his last hurry, he lugged a piece of bread so big that it blocked his vision. He ran full tilt into a fence post but he tried again. Five minutes later he was back for a second slice. Obviously he was storing provisions for the storm. As we know, squirrels are responsible for the growth of countless trees, for they never dig up all the nuts planted. But slices of bread will certainly never pop up as crusty loaves.

Several days ago, Tiny Tim at last turned up with a tiny companion. In our neighborhood, red squirrels are so scarce that he was the first one to skip along my split-rail fence. It is fascinating to see him leap along, hardly touching the rails. When he stops he sits upright, folding his paws and flicking his tail. So far our friendship has progressed so that he enjoys being talked to, but at a respectable distance. He is a merry little person, and guests laugh when they see him tugging away at a cookie as big as he is. Sunflower seeds are his preferred food, but he eats everything I put out for birds and stray cats.

Now we have a pair of red squirrels. So far the new arrival only slips in and out like a shadow, but I hope she likes the wooded area below the fence, poison ivy and all.

During the height of the vacation a good many of the smaller wild creatures are run over. So are cats and small dogs. I wonder what happens to the few moments saved by speeding drivers?

Cookouts flourish in July. Days can be hot, but as the sun drops toward the horizon, a cool air drifts in across the water. Then the charcoal grill sends that savory smoky odor over the patio or deck or across the garden, and one of Ellis's famous steaks is brought out. These days, steaks mean a special occasion but are well worth it. Hamburgers and frankfurters are in high favor too. A raw vegetable salad and chunks of garlic bread round out the meal.

The appetizers we like best are Amity Hill shrimp. This calls for 1 pound of cleaned, cooked shrimp, which you may prepare early in the day. Then you make a sauce of 1 cup chili sauce, 1 clove garlic (minced), ½ teaspoon Beau Monde (if you are not out of it), ½ teaspoon sugar, a dash of Worcestershire sauce, a dash of sherry or white wine. Dip each shrimp in the sauce and wrap in ½ slice bacon (cut as thin as possible). Secure with toothpicks. Refrigerate everything until you are ready. When you are pouring the chilled drinks, broil the shrimp until the bacon begins to crisp. (With me it always wants to slide off if I turn away.) I serve in an old-fashioned copper chafing dish, but an electric skillet does just as well and so does a wok.

Ruth Walker's liver mold is another favorite. It can be made the day before, which is an added attraction for me. It also uses ingredients easy to find in the pantry. It calls for 1 can condensed consommé, 1 envelope Knox gelatin, chopped parsley and chives to taste, 8 ounces whipped cream cheese, 1 can liver spread, 1 teaspoon lemon juice. Bring the soup to a boil and dissolve the gelatin in it. Add herbs and let cool. Mix cheese, liver, and lemon juice. Put some of the soup in an oiled bowl or mold and let it set. Put the cheese in and top with the remaining soup mixture. Chill in refrigerator. Serve on a small platter surrounded with crisp crackers. Cut in slices with a sharp knife and let the guests serve themselves.

There are always some people who do not eat liver in any shape or form. But those who enjoy the spicy, rich taste will make sure you have no leftovers. And for the misguided who shun any form of liver, Muenster or Camembert cheese, cut wafer thin and served with toasted crackers, will be satisfactory.

Summer parties do not need desserts, I think. A bowl of

cool fresh fruit topped with mint is a good ending. But my friend Martha glorifies ripe juicy cut-up fruit by serving the slices in a soft honey-colored custard sauce. Ripe strawberries, savory peaches, dark plump blueberries—almost every kind of fruit is graced by the sauce. It is not a thick, heavy, too-sweet sauce but thin and delicate so that it does not overwhelm the fruit. It is, in short, just right. It reminds me of a time in my life devoted to Floating Island, which I loved with the passion my grandchildren feel for chocolate layer cake.

Now in July, evenings are dipped in moonlight. The Mill Pond is a sleeping princess; even the tips of the junipers on the shore are still. The air smells of wild roses and honeysuckle and dewy grass. At Still Cove one or two birds utter a few notes, dreamy and sweet. I cannot decide why the scattered cheeps poke into the quiet.

For a brief time we can forget strikes, shortages, world conflicts and rest in the peace of a July night with the moon and stars in their familiar sky.

Tomorrow may be fair!

August

The Full Sturgeon Moon rises over Mill Pond with a special richness. It may be my imagination, but I feel that the color of the moon fits the month. I think of the white moon of January, the pure gold of June, and in this month the tint of orange. Experts would tell me that the month has nothing to do with it, I am sure; it is atmospheric conditions. But the colors do change on the earth below, for now rich reds, purples, blues take over. Flowers are more intense in color, as if having a last fling before the chilling frost. Thistles, chicory, asters, gladioli, goldenrod are blooming. The cranberry beds brighten. Beach plums ripen. This August runs true to form.

Less reliable is the cycle of nature in the Cape waters; there is always the fear of a lobster shortage. Lobsters now are less plentiful than they once were. For generations they have been hauled from the sea in ample supply, but not any more.

It takes seven years for a lobster to mature fully. If the bearing-age lobsters are harvested too widely, the species will be not simply endangered but extinct. We have been hovering on the edge of this crisis for some time. Now the daily topic of conversation is the price of lobster, and despite my devotion to crab, I know that the big, ungainly crustacean is the king of the sea—or queen (extra dividends with the queen)—and that protection and regulation are essential.

When we first came to the Cape, there was no Lobster Pool on Route 6A where the victims drift idly about in a clean tank of seawater. There was no enormous electric steaming equipment where your lobsters could be cooked for you, ready to be rushed home while your Irish setter jumped up and down with ecstatic tail. There may have been places on the Cape that cooked the lobsters for their customers, but if so, we did not know about them. Most of the people we met had big lobster pots in the pantry or the hall closet. We ourselves had our old canning kettle, still in good shape after years of "putting up" the garden produce.

Our first lobster was from Harry Hunt, who lived on Tonset Road near us. In front of his handsome white house was a sign saying LOBSTERS. As I remember, it did not even say "For Sale." Harry Hunt was already a legend. His lobster boat was a big beautiful deep-sea craft named Gertrude after his wife, an Eskimo girl he had met when he was on an expedition to Alaska.

The lobsters waited for their destiny in a huge crate in the corner of the garage, and we got acquainted with Gertrude when she was on duty as saleswoman. When I see her nowadays, she has not changed; she is still strong, quick-moving, bright-eyed, smiling.

The first winter I spent alone on the Cape, I came to depend on Gertrude in an unexpected way. I went daily to the post office, which was then located in the old building, at the top of a slope. In December, the parking lot was often like a skating rink. Piles of packages arrived for me at that time, especially cartons of books, which weighed tons. Somehow I was never able to find a parking space on the upper level, so I trudged fearfully up and down. If the postmaster, Howard Sinclair, was not jammed into his office, he would dash out to carry a load of cartons for me, but around the holiday season the whole staff worked like coal miners and there was no time for extra tasks. One day, I had just signed at the desk for an unbelievable load when someone touched my arm. It was Gertrude Hunt.

"Let me help," she said.

In three or four minutes she had sailed down the ice to bring up against my car. She carried enough boxes in her arms to come up to her eyebrows. Then she saw me safely out of the parking lot. This was not an isolated act of mercy, for after that she took time to be a carrier for me. Now that the post office has moved to the old Stop-and-Shop location on Main Street, the level parking makes things easier, but I will always remember the old days.

Back to that lobster borne home triumphantly from Henry Hunt's garage. I couldn't help looking at it, as it waved its claws on the kitchen counter. The lobster looked at me too. That did it. The water boiled violently in the kettle. Everyone else in the group had run down to the beach to gather some driftwood (there was plenty of it in those days) for the fireplace. I couldn't just stand there, that was evident. I was expected to *cook* that lobster. They certainly did not intend for me to keep him as a house pet. In the end, when I couldn't find a laundry bag (too big anyway), I took a brown paper bag and edged my victim into it. Then, before the thrashing had slit the paper, I shut my eyes and dropped the bag into the boiling water. I got quite a burn and the kettle steam took some of the paint from the kitchen ceiling. But the lobster got done and everybody said it was delicious. I ate frankfurters.

This is why I think one of the best services the Cape offers is steaming your lobsters to order! And cracking them too, if you wish.

A lobster dinner at day's end makes the heart light. And there's a cool wave coming!

Our quiet neighborhood is still recovering from the realization that we are not safe from the ills of our time. Snow Shore was always, to us, simply a tranquil beach below Champlain Road. Walking down the short way from Champlain to Snow Shore was a favorite twilight stroll. We also used to go swimming there when the other beaches were crowded. A few small boats anchored offshore in season. All in all, it was an idyllic place. My Irish setter, Holly, especially loved it, and I found it a particularly good spot for sitting on the sand and dreaming while she dashed into the blue water and swam full speed toward nowhere.

So when I heard the words "Snow Shore" on the faithful local radio station at eight in the morning, I wondered how such a peaceful place had hit the news. But when I heard the rest of the item, I dropped my soft-boiled egg on the counter.

"At two fifteen in the morning, three Orleans police officers made the arrest." And the story continued. Some nearby residents had heard unusual noises and called the police. One or two boats were unloading cargo on the beach. The cargo was marijuana, in bales. At the same time, in Wellfleet, an arrest was made. In all, the amount of the drugs was four and a half tons, estimated at some millions of dollars. Eleven men were arrested. The landing boat of one was hauled away to a garage, the owner held on $25,000 bail. There was one mystery girl who drove a truck to the shore and fled into the woods.

We have all known about the drug trade, as well as about the general crime wave of our period. But it is always a shock when this sort of activity turns up at your own back door.

It reminded me of the first time I came to the Cape. We rented sight unseen a cottage on Champlain Road. It was formerly the home of a pirate captain, and the woman we rented from was one of his descendants. I now see why the pirate's home was just a stone's throw away from Snow Shore. He must have moored his ship in the sheltered cove there. Did he ever unload on the same beach where the bales of marijuana were dumped?

I did not think the captain's house compared well with the sea captain's mansions such as the Linnell House or the one at Barley Neck, so perhaps his take was not what it might have been. The house was small. It had a fireplace for heat. Oil lamps lighted it. The stove was a rusty kerosene affair. We got a grill and did most of the cooking outside. There was also an outhouse bedded in poison ivy. In some houses, these features would have added to the picturesque charm and we would have enjoyed the adventure of primitive living. But somehow in this house they were merely dreary. I was disappointed that it was not furnished with a ghost, at least, but after all, a ghost could have found better quarters.

We did know that the descendant was authentic because she accused us of stealing her clothesline.

Generations have come and gone, but now tranquil Snow Shore is once more the scene of lawbreaking. However, this is a different crime. This involves smuggling a drug that particularly damages the young. The police chief was asked if the four and a half tons were destined to go across the bridge.

"Oh, no," he said. "All for the Cape."

In other words, it was not bound for ghettos in the big cities. Nor was it intended for expensive urban discos. It was for this quiet land embraced by the sea.

What can be done? The Orleans police are the finest in any place I have ever lived—which covers a big territory— and they do an incredible job of catching lawbreakers. But it seems that the only real answer to the drug problem would be lack of a market. The current profit for the confiscated crop is estimated at $250,000 for the owner of the carrier boat: not bad for one night's boatride! How do we help our young people, to say nothing of many of their elders, stay clear of this ever-present temptation? It is a question we cannot set aside any longer.

But until the drug problem is solved, we can only make our position plain and do whatever small things we can to help. Do not ignore unusual happenings in the neighborhood. Let police know. Too often we hear, "Well, I don't want to get involved. I mind my own business." But the health of our young is everybody's business.

Every night the police cruiser drives down Mill Pond Road to the town landing. He comes several times, and I watch for him. When I see the flashing lights, I wave a greeting to him even though he cannot see it. But it gives me a comfortable feeling, all the same. In spite of the problems, we are in good hands.

This is the time for cold soup. You can make it beforehand and set it in the refrigerator to chill. Put the bowls in too if you have room. Then when you ladle it out, add a touch of elegance in the garnish. One of my favorites is Colonel Edwards's Vichyssoise. I have tried many varieties of vichyssoise and like them all, but this recipe is the one I copied for my own cookbook.

I was introduced to this lovely soup on a warm southern evening when I was at the Virginia Military Institute visiting Murray Edwards, an old friend who was on the faculty. Murray cooked the dinner, and afterward we sat on the porch and watched the moon rise over the blue mountains of Virginia while we sipped the colonel's specially ground coffee. The military band was practicing, and music never sounded sweeter.

The entire meal was delicious, but the high point was the vichyssoise. It calls for 2 cups diced raw potatoes, 2 cups diced raw leeks (or onions if you have no leeks), 1 cup chicken broth, 1 cup sour cream, 1 teaspoon Worcestershire sauce, seasoned salt to taste, and chopped chives. Cook the potatoes and leeks in a very little water until soft. Press through a food mill or use the blender. Add the broth. Cool. Add the sour cream and beat well. Add seasonings and chill. Serve in chilled cups, topped with a sprinkle of chives. This is supposed to serve 4 to 5, but don't count on it.

Cape visitors who want to taste the best cold soups need only take the beach road to Barley Neck Inn. The chef there is a genius at cold soups. I thought the cream of broccoli was my favorite until last Wednesday, when he had cream of carrot and chives. I normally do not run after carrots, but that soup was elegant.

The first time I had the cold soup at Yesteryear in Eastham, it had special charm because it was served in crystal goblets with long stems and wide tops. Alas, the next time we went, the soup came in soup bowls! But it was good—cream of watercress, I think.

This was a small change, but other changes are not so minor. East Orleans is sadly changed the past few years: the magnificent old elms have been coming down. The Dutch elm disease does have a cure now, they say, but so far, cutting the dead trees seems to be the usual treatment. Sometimes the fallen lengths of trunk lie so long where they fall that I wonder if the killer bugs haven't simply moved on to a yet-healthy tree. Why not?

The drift toward autumn is slow and dreamy at first. There is no urgency. Is nature changing her pace or is it a holding back on our part? Do we really want the brisk September days which precede the storm-window reign? Or are we trying to pull back summer? Whichever it is, the rhythm changes.

"I know I ought to think about fall cleaning," I tell Amber.

She stretches out one paw full length and yawns delicately. "Plenty of time," she says.

Flowers and crops come to mature richness. Inland the

smell of corn pollen rides the air. The nesting songs of birds diminish to a soft, undramatic melody. A few summer people begin the melancholy task of bringing in boats. Some leave the boats riding a while longer on Mill Pond or Pleasant Bay or some other inlet. This gives such a good excuse to come back for a weekend. Then there are those who take late vacations at the end of the month when they hope everyone else will have gone. There were years, we remember, when the season ended at Labor Day, but now the end of October finds Main Street still crowded with off-Cape cars. And before the gas problem, there was a growing tendency for people to come and "see what winter is like on Cape Cod."

About the only treat we cannot offer in winter is skiing. But after all, the Cape is simply not mountain country, it is seacoast.

One thing I remember from my childhood in Wisconsin is the chicory blooming in August along the wooded country roads. Chicory came from Europe and was used to make a coffeelike beverage. It was also mixed with authentic coffee when the latter was hard to come by. The blossom grows on tall slim stalks and is intensely blue. The petals are fine, the size about right to make a teacup for a doll. And oh, how chicory grows—spreading a dense rippling ribbon marking the roads! It grows in New England too. In Connecticut, I tried to welcome it into the farmhouse garden but learned it did not like to be moved. There is some on the Cape but not around Mill Pond.

Wildflowers are noted for being hard to transplant. The lightest quiver upsets the hairline roots. I used to wonder whether even a well digger could move one clump of arbutus to my garden. But wildlings have their opinions about where to grow. Where the bluff descends rather modestly from our yard to Mill Pond, the land looked exactly right for wild cranberry. The soil was the same sand, the sunlight slanted down at the same angle, the amount of water was the same as on the miles lining the coast from Eastham toward Province-town. Jill, my housemate when we built Still Cove, decided that our bluff could indeed be covered with wild cranberry. It is a beautiful plant, the berries as red as the cultivated ones, the leaves a glossy green which brightens dark winter days, and the flowers ivory, flecked with pink (they remind me of arbutus).

As it turned out, almost everything else flourished on our slope except cranberries. There was plenty of ivy, for instance (where did that come from?), wild daisies, dandelions, even daffodils from the border. At various times we talked about spading up the whole area and starting over with railroad ties and calling it our stairway to the beach. But we never got around to it. Now, years later, nature has fixed everything. For although the cranberries never settled in comfortably on the slope, the lower terrace is awash with them. Obviously they find this a better place than the slope. Stu and Russ Crosby, who take care of most of the landscape business here-about, frequently shake their heads and comment on how seldom wild cranberries can be transplanted so well. But the fact is, these cranberries transplanted themselves; we just saw them move from the slope. Nowadays, to get to the beach one has to walk around this lovely spread.

I remember when goldenrod was supposed to be the cause of hay fever and this was a great pity, for goldenrod makes lovely bouquets in the house as well as lifting golden spikes along country roads. One kind is a rusty, almost coppery color, not the regular sun yellow. Fortunately, we have learned that ragweed is the true cause of hay fever, and people have stopped tearing out the prettiest of the late-summer wildflowers. I have a few friends who are still positive that goldenrod makes them sneeze, and since pollen is borne on the wind from many sources, there is no use arguing. But I myself love it, indoors and out.

The famous Cape pine pollen is best not mentioned in any conversation about allergies, however. When I see a tide of yellow powder on the front steps and the car windshield drifted thickly, I add extra boxes of tissue to my shopping list. And put off phoning the Piknicks to come and wash the Still Cove windows.

The Piknicks are an institution in our neighborhood. They not only *run* the Cape Cod Cleaning Company, they *are* the company. Mr. and Mrs. Piknick are sturdy, brisk, warm people who have been in the business of window washing ever since I first met them. They have raised three boys, all handsome, responsible, charming young men. Once, when they were in college, I was feeling very discouraged about the younger generation. It was window time, and when the Piknicks came, I was surprised to see that the boys had come too for the late-season washing.

"I thought the boys were in school," I said.

"Off for two days," Mr. Piknick said. "Football game."

I took some time to digest this. Another question revealed that they came home *every* weekend to help out the family. They never acted sullen, either: in fact, as the family worked together, any difficult spots were erased by laughter.

One time one of the boys had a face so swollen with poison ivy that it was hardly possible for him to see through a slit in his eyelids.

"How ever did you get that?" I asked, the way stupid people do.

"My father was trying to move a piece of machinery in the back of the lot, and I thought it was too heavy for him. So I dashed out without really noticing where I was walking, and it was covered with poison ivy out there."

That day the temperature was over 80 degrees, but he

worked right along with the rest, except for stopping now and then to turn the hose and plunge his face in the cool well water.

Window washing is a special art, I think, and a difficult one. My efforts have always been failures. Windows have four corners, and some have extra panes. Little blobs of dirt lodge in every angle. A razor blade is always necessary for the leftover paint that is bound to speckle the edges. The main part of the glass seems spotless when you polish it, but ten minutes later a large bluish smudge covers the area. The Piknicks station one member on each side of the window so that blurs and spots never escape. When the job is done, Mr. Piknick examines every inch of glass before they say goodbye to Amber and pile the ladders in the car.

It occurs to me that we all look at our world through glass. There is always that thin barrier between us and everyone else. The glass is our own limitations. Bias, prejudice, ignorance cloud our vision. The whole house is shining after the Piknicks go, and I decide to make the house of my spirit glow as well, by scrubbing away the accumulated impediments.

Yesterday when I came back from town, I found a basket of fresh-picked vegetables on the kitchen counter, another gift from the community garden. This year the fine open area is located on Beach Road. It must have been part of a farm and is a meadow fringed by pine woods. The plots were assigned to residents in turn, water was laid on, and the whole area marked by stakes.

One day I drove over with Olive to see how her vegetables were doing. Twenty-three days of drought and blistering heat had meant that the gardeners had worked extra hard, watering, mulching, watering, watering, watering. Nevertheless, as we parked beside Olive's plot, I could hardly believe it was real. The rows of vegetables stood proudly in long lines.

The land had returned rich bounty for the gardeners' efforts.

The tender light of twilight was moving in, but an ebbtide of sunset flowed from the west. As I watched Olive bending over a row of dense yellow beans, the whole tone of the scene was a green-blue framed by the darker green of the pines in the background. Even the kneeling figure was clad in blue pants and shirt. Then the pale golden beans came popping from their bushes. The big floppy leaves of the Brussels sprouts were a more delicate shade of green-blue. It was like a painting by one of the great French Impressionists.

Then I thought about all the places on this planet today where starvation is a matter of course. Here on Cape Cod, this one small space had produced such bounty.

In Olive's own plot were pole beans, yellow beans, Brussels sprouts, beets, cabbage, kohlrabi, turnips, tomatoes, lima beans, corn. In her back yard at home were sugar snap beans, lettuce, more tomatoes, bush beans, eggplant, cucumbers, squash, peppers. Both plots had marigolds; the home garden also had sweet peas. Marigolds were supposed to protect the crop but also make bright bouquets in the house. What a wealth of nourishment lies in the earth, and what power a handful of seeds carries in it! Why can't the brains of man, which can engineer trips to the moon, figure a way to provide the hungry with food enough for survival?

The rich crops harvested on Beach Road will be the last grown there: the area has been sold and bulldozers will be ripping it up soon. But this day Olive was gathering slender yellow beans as fast as she could pick. Of course we had no basket in the car, not even a shopping bag, so she had to fish out the day's newspaper. A newspaper, as we all know, is helpful for far more than news. Spread open, this one held a small mountain of beans, enough to share with three neighbors.

"There's a lot more," said Olive.

I found it easy to snip the beans as Olive and I were riding in the sunset. I can remember times when I have had to use a sharp knife to cut the ends of string beans, but these had been picked at just the right moment and one pinch did the trick.

We all need tranquillity, and getting close to the earth is a good way to find it. We also need balance, which is difficult. For one thing, in this age we know about the sufferings all over the world. We hear every day about the tragedy of refugees, the assassinations, the children caught up in crime or warfare. In earlier times, people were mainly involved in whatever went on in their own immediate area. Suppose we could not hear what was happening in Europe until the news came by schooner? We would still have enough to worry about on our own shores, but we might hope to cure these local evils, and hope is a vital necessity. Now that we see we are members of a worldwide community, the task is harder. All the same, I cherish the feeling that all people everywhere are my neighbors. And I wish they could all share a little of the peace and bounty that we know here.

Summer visitors who come to the Cape by plane are full of stories about the difficulties of air travel. It seems to be a neat trick to land in the same airport as your luggage. They themselves do a good deal of detouring to Boston and New Bedford because Hyannis is fogged in. When delays of various kinds are the subject of conversation, I think of Olive's experience with Aunt Hilda. She was due to land at La Guardia after a long flight in one of the big new planes. The family went over from New Jersey to meet her at the appointed time. The huge monster sliced down the sky and maneuvered to a landing.

But the passengers did not emerge. The door remained closed. A crowd began to gather, and air officials appeared. Obviously something was seriously wrong. A hijacker? A terrorist? Some of the people waiting began to shout. More people arrived.

Finally the plane doors swung open, the landing equipment was hooked up, and passengers began to file down the steps, most of them in anything but a happy mood. One of the last was Aunt Hilda, slightly flushed but composed.

After the greetings everyone spoke at once.

"What in the world happened? What went wrong?"

"I lost a package," said Aunt Hilda. "A very important package."

"You mean to say you were the one who caused all that delay? And just for a package?"

"Well, I couldn't have everybody get off until it had been found," Aunt Hilda said. "That package had the Boy Scout suit I bought at Sears in Houston for my nephew."

Her nephew was two years old.

When it is too hot to cook, even for special visitors, we are grateful for that other visitor from the city: the local delicatessen. Two years ago, a fine store opened in East Orleans. Called cosily the Deli, it is a small place, and a plain door opens directly into the shop. There are no fancy decorations, no buoys or anchors or carved birds. But oh, there is food! There is always the family, too, and it is worth going in just to visit with them. Louise manages the counter; Donna, her daughter, and Ronnie, her son-in-law, preside over the salads, meats, cheeses, manicottis, sandwiches, and staples. Ronnie has installed a butcher department with only prime meat, so that if you want to take home fork-tender chops or steaks he will cut them for you. I favor his thin slices of cold roast beef because it is rare and tender and paper-thin.

Donna's potato salad with the beef and crusty bread makes a fine supper, with fresh fruit from Fancy's stand for dessert. Or you can make a meal with one grinder from the Deli.

The roll is big and round and full of treasures: salami, cheese, pickle, pepper, crisp lettuce—I never can tell all that is in it. It varies, but it is always savory.

A good many people have started delicatessens since I first came to Cape Cod, but for various reasons they did not last long. Usually the food was excellent but the young couples were not trained in managing the business end. But Louise, Donna, and Ronnie understand the complexities of buying and selling, and we all hope the Deli will be a landmark in East Orleans as Mayo's once was. It is a comfort to know that unexpected company can be fed in short order, and no rushing about the kitchen either!

Last week's town meeting considered—but did not take a final vote on—applications for a new shopping plaza and a disco. If I had been present, I would have sided with those who spoke in favor of a slowdown in building.

Of course, Orleans cannot stand still, but progress does not always have to mean commercial expansion. Why not improve and preserve our special bit of near-paradise? We can give bulldozers and chain saws a rest and not turn our roads into speedways.

My dream would be to plant trees along the roads and let the wildflowers grow on the roadsides. Spend the funds on smooth surfaces instead of the corduroy effect now common. Tuck comfortable little rest areas here and there. I see countless young women trudging along, transporting the younger generation hunched over their shoulders and carrying groceries at the same time. How nice it would be if they could drop down on a bench under a leafy tree and plop the baby on the grass for a while.

Part of the beauty of our town comes from nature, with the sea and sand dunes framing it, and the inlets and ponds starring it. But another part comes from the architecture used in the early days. It was not only beautiful in itself but suited to the climate and the land. Now in the last few years people have begun building in Orleans residences suitable for a Florida resort or a town on the western plains. Here on the Cape, they look out of place and often downright ugly.

There are many steps that can be taken to protect Orleans and keep it a place to lift the heart. Perhaps prospective builders should have to meet with a committee on housing headed by an expert who understands the Cape and what is harmonious here. There is one house not far from our own neighborhood which we have to drive by some of the time, and although I shut my eyes, I feel the bleak mass imprinted on my eyelids. A row of these would blight even the most tranquil street.

A different sort of issue has also aroused much discussion in town meeting lately: the proposal to build a Senior Center on some gift land near Rock Harbor (what better location?). It is hard to imagine how anyone could be opposed to this. The needs of senior citizens are obvious. They do not want to miss sharing activities with others. They want a comfortable, attractive (underline that word) center where they do not have to be alone just because they can no longer go surfing or hiking miles on the beach up to their ankles in sand. Perhaps they cannot go bicycling with the rest of the family, but they should not feel like a mere fringe of society.

I began to think about all this when I visited the Brewster Senior Center recently. I began to long for Orleans to have a real center like that one, not just a place in the cellar of Town Hall. Now I believe we shall have it.

I think of a small Cape-style building with a garden where members who have none where they live can use their skills and feel kin to the earth again. Inside, a comfortable lounge with bookshelves and room for houseplants to be cared for by the members. Another room would have tables by sunny windows for cribbage or chess or jigsaw puzzles or bridge. I like to think of a man who has not had time in years for chess and now discovers a man from across town who has carved his own chess set and is ready for combat.

There should be an informal gymnasium where a skilled volunteer could help with exercises that might not be suitable for a football team but would bring new energy to stiff muscles. Properly designed bathrooms and a good kitchen are primary necessities. And so is a small room with a daybed or couch and a couple of those fancy chairs that slide up for tired feet. And I haven't yet put in a television den or a meeting room for speeches, committee battles, documentary films, maybe even book talks.

The churches and synagogues do a wonderful service for all ages, beginning with preschoolers. But their resources are just not large enough for the whole community. A town Senior Center could supplement all the existing programs.

Not just for those who are retired, either. A high percentage of older citizens work, full or part time. (I forget who first started the fixed retirement idea, but I believe this law may have a fixed retirement of its own very shortly.) Those who are employed will find that the center adds a warm glow to their lives.

Finances will be a problem for any such project, of course. But once something as valuable as this is established, people are sure to contribute for special needs. And the major accomplishment will be achieved. There will be less loneliness in Orleans.

May the additions to our town all be ones to be proud of!

My visit to the Senior Center set me to thinking about the general problems of aging in our society. As a rule, I do not pay much attention to my own stage of life, and I am startled whenever I look back over the past and realize how many years I have known. There is a cane beside the door now and an extension phone on the table near my favorite seat. The bathroom shelf holds a cluster of new pill bottles, and the kitchen calendar reminds me of my regular visits to Dr. Bill for a checkup and a dose of his healing humor. But in general, it seems to me that I am the same person I have always been. I am one of the lucky ones.

Slowly, programs are evolving to meet the needs of the older people—not just special centers like the one in Brewster but also political action groups, such as the Gray Panthers, and service programs, such as Meals-on-Wheels and Fish, the telephone and transportation network. I like the idea of using the talents of retired people in volunteer activities. There is no magic cure for anyone's ailments to match the feeling of being needed. And as for the contributions such volunteers can make, what is there to equal wisdom and experience and love?

Almost as important, it seems to me, is the sense of being in touch with the rest of the world. Now that I myself can no longer hike the great beach or sit comfortably in one of those fold-up seats at a movie or play or concert, or cope as easily as I once did with a holiday buffet for forty guests, now that it requires an effort for me to reach out to the the world, I cherish especially the occasions when the outside world comes to me.

Television is a precious link, of course, but even better are unexpected, spur-of-the-moment visits from friends, who are—I am proud to realize—of many different ages. It may be the Gibsons, with an energetic toddler and his teddy bear, or Andy Barker, here from college for a visit with his grandparents next door. Linda Toomey, who must be the busiest member of the town's young professional set (she has two jobs and all sorts of activities) nevertheless finds time to drop in at Still Cove at least twice a week to report on Dr. Kim's animal clinic, where she works at night, or on the Drama Group's latest production. Linda is a born raconteur, and I often wish for a tape recorder as she spins out one of her stories. But that would not catch her gestures, which are part of the narrative. Only a movie camera would do.

A visit from Helen Elliot and Vicky Smith invariably means a passionate discussion of education or politics or science. Theoretically, these two have given up teaching in favor of early retirement, but in fact they have simply changed locations. Now my living room is a frequent classroom. I am sure they have never had a more enthusiastic student!

When Olive comes with them, her opening remark is: "Anything around here that needs fixing?" If the answer is no, she is likely to drift off to the wing to check the bathroom faucet or the light switch, just in case. Nine times out of ten, she comes back with a smile of satisfaction. "Something told me that those screws needed tightening," she says.

Sometimes the visit is brief. "Can't stay—just dropped by to say hello." Barbara and Slim Lovely have been walking the beach and are on their way home. But the length of the stay doesn't matter, although I admit to being the sort of hostess who keeps urging her guests to have one more bite of cheese before they go; what matters is that they have stopped in even for a few minutes.

Or Pret Barker will appear in the doorway. "Could you use some flounder?" he will ask, holding out a packet of fresh-caught fish, ready for the pan. Or his wife, Kay, may turn up with the first tea rose from her garden.

In summer, many of the visitors are new to me, people who have become friends through my books and their letters. Amber has learned to sense when an inexperienced guest is about to hold the door open long enough for an alert kitten to whisk outside. But after several crises, in which she vanished into the brambles and refused to come out, a sign has been put up, asking people to be careful. So far, the warning has worked. Amber still has her outings but only on a leash.

All this coming and going keeps me in touch. And even the telephone, which is not exactly my favorite piece of house-

hold equipment, brings in the outside world. My cousin Rob distrusts the phone almost as much as I do, but his wife, Bebe, talks as comfortably into a plastic mouthpiece as she does in person, and she often calls with family news or a report on the latest town meeting. Sunday night brings my weekly call from Connie, always timed to come just after *Masterpiece Theatre* on television. Our conversation begins with a minute critical analysis of the current week's episode: plot, dialogue, direction, acting, even the settings. Then we go on to less important matters.

If I were to draw a lesson here, it would be: Reach across the miles, across the years. Keep in touch—with family, friends, life itself.

These are long thoughts for the summer season, but August is a good time for reflecting. Now at this season there is a strange feeling in the air.

The main remark is, "Where did summer go?" Nobody ever has the answer. It went with the drifting rose petals, the buttercups in the lawn, the hydrangeas billowing with deep blue balls. It went with the blackbird's *okalee, okalee,* the catbird's miau, the mockingbird's melody.

It went with the smell of honeysuckle, of new-cut grass, of sun-warmed pines. It went with sea fogs and high tides and misty moons.

September is now slipping in with the first tinge of red on a swamp maple leaf.

Summer will be folded away in memory.

September

Now in September the rhythm of life changes. Summer's lease, as Shakespeare said, hath all too short a date. The air is soft, seductive; twilights are dreamy; at night, stars candle the sky. Gardens still bloom; there will be some roses until the black frost. The Cape goldenrod spreads rusty gold along winding roadsides. Hal Borland once counted the blossoms on the sweet goldenrod that grows inland and came up with 3,023 in one spray. Here the flower heads are even denser and darker, sturdy against the sea winds.

But two main changes take place. Gardeners rush to pick the late corn, bring in summer squash, harvest the crisp string beans, and fill the salad bowl with the last lettuce and green pepper. They discover that fried tomatoes in cream gravy have not lost their charm. A few dig potatoes the size of marbles and make a whole meal of new potatoes doused in milk, butter, seasoned salt, and pepper. The state of the beach plums is the main topic of conversation.

The second change is the end-of-summer migration across the bridge. Cars are crammed with children, dogs, luggage, sleeping bags, boxes of shells still smelling of the sea, and sometimes bicycles, canoes, and fishing gear precariously lashed on the cartop or hanging behind in a trailer. School is just ahead, so fathers and mothers haul reluctant sun-brown children from the beach, catch the family pet (who vanished as soon as he heard the word "suitcase"), turn in the keys for the rented cottage.

"Do we really have to go back so soon? Why can't we stay a little longer?"

"You have to go to the dentist before school opens, remember. And you have to have new shoes." Besides, Daddy has to get back to work, in many cases Mommy does too; at the very least, she has plenty of household chores to attend to before everybody is settled in for autumn.

It is a melancholy procession, bumper to bumper all the way to the canal, where the bridge writes the final signature of Cape Cod against the pale September sky.

Now the year-round residents have the Cape to themselves. All during July and August, they have looked forward to the comfortable life-style. You can go to town and actually find a place to park. You get waited on at the market right away. Shopping is simple and everything is on sale, especially bathing suits, beachwear, summer slacks. It is even possible to get a table at a restaurant without standing in line. Nauset Beach will not have to be closed because there is not room for one more automobile. There is plenty of parking space to watch sunsets at Rock Harbor. People walk slower. Streets absorb the quiet.

However, a strange thing happens. We begin to feel sad for the travelers who are leaving. Those children who found freedom running in the sand, splashing in the clean water, hunting shells, flying kites, are now *going away!* Parents who dug clams, launched small boats, walked the White Cedar Trail, visited the Audubon Center, are going back to daily responsibilities, set routines, eternal clock-watching. Many will also have to take up heavy social schedules again: no more casual picnicking or meals any old time when the clams are dug or the children come in from a last dip in the ocean.

We sit in the yard sipping cool drinks and watching the long shadows lattice the lawn.

"Now we can get back to regular living," says Jan Krusen.

"Finally! But you know, I'm going to miss the Lawsons," Linda says. "I wish Indiana were near enough so they could come here for Thanksgiving."

"I had some good fishing with Butler," Bob Gibson puts in. "And the children are mooning around driving us crazy because the Pryers are gone."

"Most of the summer people are very nice," Kay Barker sums up. "It's easier without them, of course. But somehow, I'm sad when they cross the bridge."

Now and then, the annual trek loses some of its regular participants. This year, the three teachers from New Jersey have decided to take early retirement and stay on the Cape. So Helen and Vicky will be at Holly Hill when frost comes, and Olive will not miss the fall flowers in her garden at Topside. As for me, I will be spared all the anguish of saying goodbye.

Now that Topside will be open on a year-round basis, Olive can make long-range plans. She is talking of adding a wing, expanding the garden. But her first move was to add to the household. Fergus was twelve weeks old when he bounced into the small house on the corner of Mill Pond Road. He is a Cairn, as Scotch as kilties. His ancestors did not come on the *Mayflower;* they were natives of the Isle of Skye: sturdy, small terriers with practical rough coats, pixie faces, ears standing up like sails in a brisk breeze, bright china-button eyes, and tails that never stopped wagging.

His new home was already ruled with firm paws by Boy, a regal Siamese who had been in charge ever since kittenhood, and by the king's second-in-command, a so-called "American shorthair" who blew in during a blizzard when he was a black morsel, starving and with no papers under his arm. A weaker kitten might not have survived, but this one quickly earned himself the name of Spunky and grew into a handsome adult, thick-furred and black as night.

When Fergus arrived, Topside began to resemble one of those international confrontations in which nobody ever agrees with anybody, arguments pour like Niagara Falls, and nationals go home to increase defense budgets and invent new nuclear weapons.

The deposed king promptly vanished. As every cat lover knows, a cat can seem to dissolve into thin air: downstairs, upstairs, into bureau drawers, onto top cupboard shelves, even inside an open washing machine. After a frantic search, Boy was finally located under a bed in the former attic, now a dormer bedroom. Spunky chose the puckerbush in the farthest corner of the yard. He retreated there and refused to emerge. In short, they acted like human beings. Fergus, meanwhile, behaved like the canny Scot he was. He busied himself with toys, tumblers, socks, stolen bits of watermelon. Cats? What cats? He didn't see any cats.

Before long, the ebullient puppy had charmed the neighbors as he tried to soar like a plump butterfly or bounced after balls, laddered himself into laps, gobbled up the cats' food (and promptly threw it up again on the new living-room rug), and generally focused attention on himself. The cats eventually condescended to rejoin the household, but only at a distance—they still hissed, showed their claws, and swelled up into furry balloons. Fergus quickly learned that they were not toys or other puppies.

Fortunately, the small cosmos is presided over by a mistress who is a rare diplomat. The public adulation of Fergus was quieted, Boy invited to all visiting laps, Spunky mollified with extra tidbits of roast beef. Fergus was persuaded to nap in the bedroom while the cats had a turn center stage.

By now, some weeks later, cautious sniffing has begun: the tentative advance to détente. And unlike human détente, this one, when it comes, will be something to depend on. Acceptance and understanding will follow.

We are often told that cats and dogs cannot live together.

This did not bother my family when we had a bevy of cocker spaniels, three Irish setters, and two cats. One of my favorite photographs shows a honey-colored cocker asleep in the armchair by the fire with her paws folded comfortably about a sealpoint Siamese. The Manx and one Irish always claimed the sofa, and the humans took what was left over.

My friend Laura Griffith sets out an evening meal on the back step for a rabbit, a skunk, her collie, and two barn cats. Fergus, Boy, and Spunky have not yet reached this stage of harmony. Still, they do eat at the same time nowadays, although Boy dines elegantly on the kitchen table, Spunky briskly polishes off his own dinner on the counter next to the sink, and Fergus happily slurps and whooshes on the floor.

Watching the Scot, the Siamese, and the American shorthair working their way toward peaceful coexistence and perhaps even friendship, I wonder why mankind cannot do as well. Suppose we could get to know one another—not on the battlefields or at long, futile conferences but in quiet places as individuals. Perhaps then peace would not be just a transient visitor but would finally come to stay.

Speaking of visitors who come to stay reminds me of the Canada geese. For several days now they have been fishing in the part of Mill Pond that is opposite my bedroom window. This is unusual since their favorite spot is the place this side of the town landing where a freshwater spring comes in. They must have followed a school of small fish over to this side. It is like watching a ballet to see the long dark necks curve down into the water in graceful rhythm. Toward dusk they draw autumn's symbol in the sky, the V of flight to the north. But some of them will simply circle the cove and come back again: more and more, part of the flock is wintering over on Mill Pond.

They get along amiably with the other waterfowl. All sorts of ducks and gulls sail calmly among the geese, who ignore them completely or act as if they were not there at all—

which is one way to avoid conflict, I suppose. Somehow I like the Topside approach even better.

Not long ago I saw another sort of confrontation which had a happy ending. It took place late at night in the yard at Still Cove, and it involved, of all things, a skunk.

For at last I have a skunk again! He must be a descendant of Blackberry, who built his burrow below the rail fence on the slope. Since Blackberry died, his path up the hill has grown over in a tangle of vines and briars. His feeding bowl is gone from the yard, and no plump form has ambled to the door to knock if dinner is late. But one night a couple of weeks ago, just as Linda was leaving, she started back when she opened the front door.

"Gladys, your skunk has come back," she said. "Or at least, it looks just like him. You have another Blackberry!"

There he was, bumbling about the birdbath. The white blaze was exactly like Blackberry's, wide and deep, as if he had just shrugged into an ermine jacket. At the sound of Linda's voice, he backed down the hill, taking the same route his predecessor used.

For several nights after that, he was not visible, but last night he came back. Fortunately there was a pan of scraps on the ground near the birdbath. Three or four neighbors were sitting in the living room sipping cool drinks, and since it was one of those summery nights we often have in September, Helen decided to open the front door for the breeze.

"He's here!" she said in a stage whisper.

An instant audience gathered to peer at him, entranced, as he gobbled the choicest morsels. Then suddenly, another guest appeared—one of the most spectacular of the wildlings, a big raccoon, sleek and agile. His black mask was turned toward the skunk.

The skunk stopped eating, stamped his front feet sharply in the traditional first warning, and raised his tail to defensive position. The raccoon retreated, advanced, stepped back,

stood still. We waited for the combat. I could see that Helen was tightening her grip on the door, ready to slam it shut if the skunk fired.

A moment later, two heads were bobbing into the food bowl side by side. Skunk and raccoon ate in perfect amity. At the last, the raccoon grabbed the dish and pranced off with it, dropped it, seized it, and swung it around again. It was a dance, no doubt about it. The skunk looked around as if wondering where the food pan had vanished. Then he dropped his nose to the grass and began poking about for a few last crumbs. Catching sight of him, the raccoon decided to do the same.

The drama was over and the moon was high above Mill Pond. The guests felt that they must go home. How fortunate to have the kind of friends who do not want to disturb the wildlife in the yard! Carefully Helen and Vicky tiptoed out the wing door, at the side of the house, and crept along the far edge of the drive. Unfortunately, there is no way to quiet a starting car.

"Never mind, he'll be back," said Olive.

"He did *not* panic," Linda said. "It was as if he thought, 'Oh, well, if that's the way they feel. If they want me to go, I might as well.' "

I am sure she is right. And tomorrow I will set out a double meal.

Most of us on the Cape do not find it silly to care about the creatures who live here with us. Raccoons can be a nuisance, of course, because they are able to open even the most tightly latched garbage can, and they never clean up after themselves. But when a pair sit on the split-rail fence in your front yard, their luxuriant fur shining in the moonlight, their little bandit faces turned to the house in hopes of leftovers, most people hereabouts have a feeding dish ready. To watch a raccoon pick up a piece of bread with his hands and eat it as a person does is a delight—even though he has the table manners of a hungry four-year-old.

Skunks are welcome, too. Some of them become quite tame. Blackberry not only scratched at the door when he was hungry, he also knew the sound of my car and poked his head over the bank to greet me; he whisked into the bayberry bushes when a strange car pulled in. There were no difficult encounters with dogs, since Blackberry's schedule was always predictable. The neighbors simply made sure that Rover was indoors from ten thirty to eleven every night.

When the skunk epidemic swept the Cape, my phone rang daily.

"Our two skunks are gone," Barbara said. "We haven't seen either of them for over a week. I was wondering about Blackberry."

"He hasn't come around lately either," I said. "But I'm sure he'll show up tonight." However, when the path to his burrow closed in, I had to admit that he was gone.

Now, at last, another skunk has come. I think I will call him Moondust.

Another attraction at Still Cove is a young rabbit who goes up and down the steps to the beach instead of cutting straight down the bank. No stage star ever had a more delighted audience than this one rabbit. The steps are high for his small person and take a lot of hopping, but he prefers them all the same.

Now that autumn is at hand, the furry folk are beginning to prepare for winter. It is a farewell to summer, and there is always a sadness about farewells.

The birds, too, are feeling restless. Before long some of them will be starting on the long trek south. Others are eating as if every meal might be their last, building up stamina to survive the cold season here in the North. Those who live in this neighborhood will never need to worry about going hungry, no matter what the weather, but even if they have a faint memory of finding cracked corn miraculously strewn on top of last winter's snowdrifts, instinct urges them to eat everything possible right now.

I am always surprised when city visitors look out the big window and say, "What are those birds at the feeder?" I ought to remember my own days in New York, when all I could see from our narrow apartment window was an occasional pigeon or sparrow.

"That one is a yellowthroat," I answer. "And the one emptying the birdbath is a mockingbird. He's an obsessive washer. Must be the cleanest bird on the Cape."

"Oh, look! There's a whole crowd of plump little birds scurrying by the fence."

"Those are the quail. There should be twelve—I wonder why we only have eleven today. In courting season, you know they are coming because you can hear the *bob white* call, but nowadays they don't have much to say. They're after the cracked corn. And one of them likes to take a dust bath under the rosebush."

"How do you know all this? You must have read every bird book in print."

"Well, no, it's just that after you've lived with birds for a while, they seem like members of the family."

When new people move to the Cape from city living, they have to get used to hearing the long-term residents spend half the time at a party discussing who has which birds—"Was that really a great horned owl?"—and what they feed them—"Thistle seeds cost a fortune these days"—or when the migratory ones are due to leave or arrive. The Cape is, of course, famous as a way station for migrators—one might say for the human as well as the winged species.

The next thing we know, the new residents turn up at Snow's for bird feeders along with the inevitable bath mats, shower curtains, and shelf paper. Bird books *are* helpful, and the Compass Rose Book Shop carries Peterson's classic guide, which is the basic text for fledgling bird-watchers and general reference for everybody else, as well as volumes on seabirds and shorebirds for more advanced students. (I saw a green heron today!)

Telephones are busy when the Canada geese begin to fly over in the long, mysterious, triangular pattern. As the travelers settle down on the bay to rest, you can hear them arguing. Why stop here? Why not keep going to that other inlet? This place is fine; stop complaining.

Before long they have quieted down and can turn their attention to catching a meal. There is always good fishing on Mill Pond.

The Harvest Moon has as much mystery for me now as it ever did, even though I know that the astronauts left a golf ball there. Like most tourists, they left other debris too, but when I look out over Mill Pond, I do not think of this at all. I think of mankind looking with awe at this reminder of the vastness of the universe. What the cavemen thought, we cannot know, but the wonder must have filled their hearts, and so it does ours today.

The lucent gold path on Mill Pond makes me sure I could walk across it. On the far side, lights from the new houses on what was once Mayo's Duck Farm send glimmering reflections on the dark water, and the thin, pale-gold thread of beach outlines the curve of the shore.

Cape Codders appreciate the beauty of their own place. No workman, delivery boy, or trooper checking his route ever fails to stand in the front yard and look out.

"Quite a view you have here!"

"Beautiful place this is."

"Guess you don't want to do anything much but sit and enjoy it."

Stu Crosby may be bent double, digging or planting, but when he stands up to mop his face, he looks out at the little boats riding at anchor, watches the sweep of the hawk over the big pine, sees the kingfisher tilted on a juniper tip. I have read a good deal about Cape Codders, but seldom about this appreciation of nature.

People here also cherish the past—or at least most of us do. When the old Snow's Store was torn down to make way for that impressive modern building, I made no secret of my dismay. I felt Orleans would never be the same and I said so, even in print. As a result, the day Harry Snow came to call, I couldn't help feeling a bit nervous. A big, handsome man, outstanding as a community leader, he came in and sat down by the picture window like an old friend.

"We all felt sad about the store," he said. "Snow's has been in the family for so many years. I worked there when my grandfather owned it. In those days, you know, we even carried clothes—almost everything except meat and vegetables. But the old building just gradually wore out, and finally it couldn't be shored up any longer. We hadn't much choice. But we do miss the old place, so I know how you feel."

"Nobody who shopped there will ever forget it," I told him. "It was like treasure hunting, climbing over all those cartons in the cellar when you wanted to find a lamp, or poking around upstairs in the dry goods section when you needed material for kitchen curtains. And somehow, you always found just the shade of blue you were looking for."

"Yes," Mr. Snow said, "I know."

"Still, the people there now are just as nice," I said. "Your son will go to any trouble to help if the dishwasher gets emotional, and I'm sure Mr. Duphinney missed supper the last time he had to come and poke around under our refrigerator."

Harry Snow laughed. "Well, as long as the spirit doesn't change," he said, "we're all right."

The past few years have seen many other changes in our town. The new post office is a blessing. The Double Dragon has brought delicious Chinese-Polynesian meals. A new housing unit has gone up in back of Nickerson's, and my friend Martha, who moved in as soon as it opened, praises everything from the elegant oven (in which she bakes huge batches of cookies) to the woodsy view from her picture window.

But in addition to all these, there is another talked-of change. The familiar A&P closed its doors, with the announcement that Ellis's Market would move into the building. The news was as astounding as if we'd heard that the Rock of Gibraltar was shifting to a new location.

Ellis's has been a landmark in Orleans as far back as memory goes. It began as a small country store on Cove Road. Even when we knew it thirty years ago, there was no place to park. The display windows were filled with ancient iron kettles, wooden bowls, painted spice boxes, everything but spinning wheels (at least I never saw one there). Inside, customers threaded their way around sacks of Maine potatoes, baskets of apples, tubs of dill pickles. On the shelves, S. S. Pierce (most people pronounced it "Perse" in the old way) stood next to imported mustards and jars of Cape Cod beach plum jelly and wild honey from local beehives. Twice a week there were fresh-baked brownies and round plump loaves of Portuguese sweet bread.

Lloyd Ellis was famous for his meat department, and customers came from Truro, Wellfleet, and Brewster for the thick juicy steaks, tender legs of lamb, rosy prime ribs, freshly ground lean beef. Gordon and Sarah Parent and Ruth Wilson presided over the store (Gordon always wore a straw hat), and there was always time to chat. If a customer had been ill, Lloyd was apt to say, "If ever you can't get to town and find you need something, just call up and I'll bring it over after work—even if it's only a loaf of bread." He also had a habit of "just dropping off some surplus" for a needy family. And for letting bills run on when fishing was poor.

The newest owner, Jerry Evans, has done his best to cope with a skyrocketing population and increasing inflation. He showed his care for customers by starting a delivery service. But there was no room in the old store for expansion, so it was inevitable that he would decide on larger quarters. When he moved, Ruth came with him; some of the others retired. He will need a much larger "crew" now. We all wish him great success and hope that new traditions will begin on Main Street. And we welcome the news that the old building may not be torn down but instead may be converted into a fish market, selling only seafood from local waters, caught by local fishermen.

But there will always be nostalgia for the old-fashioned country store on Cove Road, where the aisles were so crowded that we had to walk sideways—and come early before the homemade squash rolls, fresh apple pie, and blueberry muffins still warm from the oven were all snapped up!

Many of the town businesses continue as always, just where they have always been. There is Jimmy DeLory's service station, the Compass Rose Book Shop, Watson's Department Store, Brownie's Auto Repairs. We still feel that our town is not a commercial conglomerate but our own domain. And we are blessed with the special heritage of the ancient cemetery right in the middle of the business district. With its worn headstones dreaming under leafy trees, it is a testament to the past we cherish and, God willing, always shall.

Newcomers do not always have this sense of community. I heard recently of a man in Chatham who chopped down 150-year-old trees to improve his view. He had no idea that on the Cape we cherish trees. And the new property owners in this area who propose to set up gates, cutting off the beach where the old French cable building stood, have no Cape background. They do not realize that it is not their beach; it belongs to the whole community.

It takes time for some of the new settlers to adopt our way of life. But it is a way which has brought people across the bridge for many years. I hope that the latest influx will eventually merge with the longtime patterns and cherish the Cape for what it has always been, a quiet land, in harmony with sky and sea.

October

The Full Hunter's Moon of October hangs golden and serene. The clear air has a faint scent of wood smoke—from the chimney, not from a burning pile of leaves in the front yard. Nowadays, these go to the dump. But still the air smells as if there were an Indian campfire nearby, belonging to those long-ago hunters who gave this moon its name.

This is the season of abundance, so why is it always a surprise, as if we had never known such a gift? Well, at least we are not like the granddaughter of friends of mine. At great effort her grandparents took her across country to see America the Beautiful. That is, they made all sorts of plans and then started out. Their first stop was Niagara Falls. They stood spellbound, looking at the majestic cascade.

"Isn't it wonderful?" Grandma asked.

The granddaughter nodded politely. "Is it OK if I go back to the motel now and watch TV?"

The next day they flew her home and went on by themselves to the Grand Canyon.

I have never heard anyone on Cape Cod say, "Oh, well, it's just October."

There is time now to walk the beaches and listen to the sea. Tides and waves continually change the outline of the coast, reminding us that the narrow land is part of the whole mystery of nature. The tawny sand itself, as we know, resulted from millions of years of rock being ground by the inevitable powers that perhaps only geologists can visualize. Nature's history is written in every grain that we brush from our jeans. When we look out over the water, we know we are looking toward Spain, beyond the horizon. The water is now almost black-blue—perhaps cobalt is the nearest definition. Sometimes the sky is islanded with clouds moving with the wind. More often in October the sky is like an upside-down sea.

How infinitesimal our human problems, anxieties, griefs seem! We get so involved with our lives, but simply being walkers on the sand brings a new perspective. The immensity of the sea gives life itself new meaning. Perhaps it has become a cliché to say all this, but the experience never loses its power.

When the light lengthens, we decide to go home. A favorite Cape remark is, "I'd better go home and check." Not check anything specific—just check.

My feeling is that after a visit with eternity, we need to go back to our own finite selves, regain our personal identity. Along Beach Road supper lights glow in the dusk-dark. The sound of voices welcomes us, and when we turn down Blue Rock Road, Still Cove is there, tangible evidence of our own existence.

"Let's have a fire in the fireplace," says Olive, as she drops her soggy shoes. (Somehow, she always manages to get in the water.)

For the hearth is the symbol of mankind's belonging on this mysterious planet!

October drives are leisurely, the byways of the Cape quiet. The summer cottages are closed and have a waiting look. The air is still: no children's voices, no dogs' barking, no rock-and-roll slicing the stillness, no lawn mowers whirring. In year-round neighborhoods, the morning school bus rumbles past cars taking adults to work. But even so, life seems to move at a more leisurely pace at this time of year. The sound of summer deafens the ears, but now the quiet sings autumn's song.

With the roads empty we can drift along past the newer houses but stop to study the old places: the half houses, the three-quarter ones, the occasional Greek Revival mansions. As we come near the sea, we recapture the charm of sea-captains' homes with widow's walks on the rooftops. Some recent historians, I know, claim that the small, fenced-in platforms were never used as lookouts, but I prefer to side with the traditional belief. How many women left with a bevy of youngsters climbed up to those widow's walks to look to the horizon, just in case a special full-rigged ship might sail against the sunset? Nowadays some of the early bays have been filled and the houses seem stranded inland, far from the water. But even today, a tall sail could be seen from their rooftops.

We wonder about the few hardy wives who sailed with their husbands—three months, six months. They left warm stoves, clean pure water, filled pantries, feather beds, and they left neighbors. What did they think of when great storms battered those wooden hulks, iced the masts? When the salt pork was rancid, the flour maggoty, did they weep for a bowl of steaming clam chowder or a fragrant dried-apple pie? Or was it enough when the captain came to the murky belowdeck to let the icicles melt from his beard as he swallowed a mug of applejack? We shall never know, but we admire their courage.

The successful whalers, those who survived, brought home treasures, from foreign carved chests to Chinese bowls. Their mansions were built for generations; children and grandchildren prospered. If we leave the car and stroll through an arching whalebone gate into an old-fashioned garden, we walk into the memory of that time. We can almost smell

the driftwood—so much sweeter than our modern logs—
burning on the captain's hearth with its andirons shaped like
dragons.

If we drive as far as Provincetown at sunset, the long rolling
dunes take us even farther back in time. To be sure, the
great forest that once covered this whole area has vanished;
scraggly wind-bitten pines are left. But the sky is empty and
the October beaches are deserted.

The best way to see Provincetown itself is to get lost, which
Olive and I did last week. At sunset we drove along Route
6 where the long dunes billow against the horizon. Lavender
shadows on the lee sides gave a delicate color. When we
reached Provincetown, it seemed to me the summer town
had been lifted up and carried away, leaving a real small
seaport. Fortunately we took a wrong turn and in consequence
spent an hour driving up and down narrow streets, one above
the other, circling the headland. The houses are all built close
to the streets there and close together, some with cobblestone
paths leading to the gardens in the back yards. The town
was built to face the bitter winter winds, and looking at the
way the buildings are tucked low into the sandhills, today's
modern architecture seems like a bad mistake. The lower
streets that day were gilded with sunset. The shops, art galler-
ies, craft emporiums were all boarded up. We saw an occasional figure idling toward the pier. The streets are so narrow,
I was glad only three cars were parked there. When we finally
reached our destination, I felt we had been in a faraway past.
But we were back in Orleans before the moon was halfway
across Mill Pond.

A drive to Fort Hill is a special treat. The road turns up
the hill off Route 6. We go past the Penniman House, a
big Victorian mansion painted a glaring mustard yellow. It
is closed now, but I am sure the enormous blank windows
have ghosts staring at us.

Coming back to Still Cove, there is another happiness, the

feel of homing. A warm welcoming kitten yawns as she jumps in my lap.

"You've been gone long enough," she says.

Nowadays the radio informs us when the first white frost will come. But the best way to find out is by consulting a true Cape Codder. He is intimate with weather. He reads the winds, the tides, the sky; the way the seabirds fly; even the way the squirrels, rabbits, quail, and leftover flies act. But I think it is more than knowledge based on study and observation. People who live close to nature seem to have instinctive knowledge of weather.

And never underestimate the New England homemaker. All of a sudden, one balmy October day, the rhythm of household life changes. Now extra blankets blossom on clotheslines, small rugs bask in the sun, lawn furniture sneaks away to garage or cellar, floors glow from extra waxing. Those frilly white curtains are "done up" again. And those drapes tacked to a valance board across the top of the picture window really have to be cleaned.

As for closets! Always the last holdout, they are in for it now. Cleaning and sorting involves several trips to the Salvation Army depot, to the dump. The last summer clothes are lugged to a different closet, winter garments hung up to replace them. All sorts of lost treasures are suddenly found. (How did the missing red belt manage to curl itself up in the remotest corner behind the old tennis racket?)

Emergency supplies must be replenished. November storms will surely cut off "the electric." The oil lamps are empty (six days with no current last winter, remember?), and they need new wicks. The flashlight batteries have died quietly by themselves, as always. The Sterno cans are empty too. Most of the candles guttered out during summer parties, when they added a romantic touch to hamburgers and paper plates. Finally, kindling and good logs must be brought in.

Having been stranded once with an empty fireplace, this is a top priority for me.

The question of stocking the pantry now is the main subject of conversation with the neighbors. When the great storms come, will we find the shelves full of green olives, assorted patés, and potato chips?

What all this means is that one morning—in the midst of what Emily Dickinson's friend Helen Hunt Jackson called October's "bright blue weather"—we wake up knowing that the time has come to make everything shipshape for winter. I am reminded of old farmhouses in Connecticut where the foundations were thickly packed with evergreen branches to cut down those bitter drafts. I think salt hay may still be used here on the Cape.

In one way the birds are fortunate. They build their nest, lay the delicate eggs, and manage to sit on them without smashing. Then they work madly to feed the squalling youngsters. But when the nest is empty they fly away from it. Empty nests are the symbol of summer's end. When the birds come back next season, they may settle in the same place, but for most of them, the nest will be new. We keep working on the same nests.

However, when the house is snugged in, we feel triumphant.

"Now let's have one more picnic on the outer beach," says a neighbor. "It's such a lovely day."

And it is still October, bright and beautiful!

This is the time of year when New England casts a spell over the country. It is also when I get mail asking me to tell the writers exactly when is the best time to come to see the fall colors.

"We want to come when they are at their peak!"

Even the naturalists cannot predict just when autumn decides to splash hills and valleys with scarlet, gold, and russet.

The theory once was that frost caused the leaves to turn, but the leaves never paid attention to that. Now there is a new theory which has to do with the sap, some chemical change. I don't know whether the mysterious hormones have anything to do with it. I simply know it is another of nature's miracles, perhaps the most exciting. All colors seem more intense: the sapphire of the sky, the blue of the sea, the fire red of the maples, the copper of the oak. It is all dazzling, yet there is a sense of wistfulness because it is like a farewell party for a traveler starting on a long journey. Blossoming summer is the traveler, and saying goodbye is never as easy as we thought it would be.

It is travel time for the Cape Codders too. They feel like adventuring across the bridge. New Hampshire, Vermont, Maine have more deciduous trees and more mountains heavily wooded, and they flame with color. But those of us who stay home do not want any pity, for the mellow tones of the Cape landscape are beautiful, and the ocean, ponds, inlets frame every view with shining blue.

At breakfast, I look out to say good morning to my own oak tree. When I first wrote about it, there was a small twisted sapling ready for the dump. Now I have to look up to see the tip. The branches are wide-spread and deep with leaves. When Stu Crosby comes to put the roses to bed, we take time to admire it.

"Good we saved it," he says.

One special pleasure I have all during the autumn is to watch this tree. In late summer, the dark glossy green leaves begin to have a pinky look around the serrated edges—very faint at first but deepening soon as if the painter has dipped his brushes in the pot again. In October, the whole tree is like a tapestry. The center of the leaves is still green, but the green diminishes as the rosy color increases. The miracle is that the change cannot be observed. Does it always happen in the night? Or are human eyes not sensitive enough to perceive it?

By November, the green will be tucked away as if it were folded up and stored for the winter. Most of the trees will have long since sent their leaves drifting down, but my oak will still keep firm hold on hers. As I look out the window I will see that my oak is polished copper, every single leaf shining in the sunlight. But for now, it keeps October's fire. A small sapling that pokes up through the sod follows the color pattern, all six or seven leaves. I hope Tiny Tim planted an acorn from the bigger tree. If I ask him, he will not remember. For it is the forgetfulness of squirrels that built many of our forests.

At the foot of the tree, my little brown rabbit sits quietly in the warm sunlight. He is not nibbling the dried grass, he is just sitting, ears motionless, whiskers still. Do rabbits ever daydream? His gaze seems to be fixed on Mill Pond. Perhaps, like me, he enjoys the view. Or perhaps he is storing up memories of sun and mild air before the dark, cold season comes. I do that too.

Now that the new season of television is under way, I find I can still be astounded. The commercials are stupefying. There is a higher scream level in the women and an ungodly arrogance in the wonder children who adore brushing their teeth and would die for X-brand cereal that squeaks. The men are so stupid about the perfect razor or irresistible masculine perfume that it is all the seductive wives can do to put them on the right track.

I hope foreign nations do not form their ideas of us by our commercials!

I may be wrong, as I often am, but I imagine the men and women who compose these commercials could do better if only they had a freer hand.

I also find it discouraging at this moment to accept the fact that the forecasters were right when they began to tell us that the new television season was going to be worse than the last. How can this be? It turns out to be easy. Simply use reruns or spin-offs or second-rate movies dating back to the time when twenty-five cents was the price of admission and popcorn was five cents a bag. I feel sure there are new writers with new ideas; certainly life is full of material. It is as if the networks operate under a blanket of fear—never try anything new! I would think the executives might take a look at *M.A.S.H.* and *Barney Miller,* which shine like nuggets. These programs always have fresh, delightful innovations on their basic themes: "War is a bad business" and "Police staffs are human beings."

Since television is a universal force and exercises such staggering power, it seems a pity that hours of prime time are, quite simply, junk.

But PBS is an example of what can be done. If there were only one channel on the air, it should be this one. The only problem here is that they seem to spend half the time raising money to keep it going.

With all its faults, I love television. Sitting in my quiet living room, I see the national leaders as they meet. I watch refugees and rioters. I hear the voices of Russian officials and British prime ministers and Chinese premiers. I can even judge our senators by watching them on news shows. I share evenings with the Boston Symphony, opera with Beverly Sills, ballet with Baryshnikov. For sports, I have the Olympics, and I reflect that watching hockey, tennis, baseball, and football on my TV screen is far better than perching on hard bleachers so high above the field that it is almost impossible to follow everything that happens.

As I have said a good many times, there is one answer to those who hate television because of the commercials. It isn't necessary to have a remote-control device. For my own viewing times, I keep a note pad, some stationery, and a book easy to dip into beside me. During intermissions and half-times or whenever there are four or five commercials in a row, I make lists, write notes, read a page or two. If I am fairly well caught up with these, I enjoy a crossword puzzle. This way I can sit calmly through even the ads for sleep aids.

Now, I think, radio is coming into more and more favor. Radio fits in anywhere. The last time Still Cove was shingled, a small radio, resting on the grass, played music while the tomtom of hammers beat in the shingle nails. At noon the news and weather came on while the crew opened their lunches and sat comfortably around the small box.

Few homemakers nowadays clean refrigerators, scrub pans, or chop vegetables without having a radio on the kitchen counter nearby. Our local radio does a fine job of covering what is happening on the Cape. Anyone who drives back and forth learns to keep the car radio tuned in. One day I heard that a truckload of furniture had spilled on Route 28 near Chatham, so I took other roads and made my appointment on time. There are a number of interesting feature programs too. And when a hurricane moves toward Miami, we can follow its course. Will it turn westward or follow the coast to New England? (I can't get worked up about calling hurricanes by masculine or feminine names. But wait till they start to call a sailboat Harold.)

The one criticism I have of radio developed this week. I like to type with soft music (not Muzak) in the background. But I cannot enjoy "Mama don't want me, Daddy don't want me" sung in rasping voices all day long. The platter spinners' passion for this tedious number must have a reason. Could it be that someone is subsidizing it? How much would it cost to replace "Mama don't want me" with a John Denver song or "The Green Leaves of Summer"? And the ungrammatical insistence on *don't* instead of *doesn't* is no help to good English.

October weddings have much in common with the June variety. They are seldom without problems. A short time ago one was scheduled here in Orleans at the Church of the Holy Spirit. This is the most beautiful sanctuary imaginable. It reminds me of churches in English villages, set back from the road and with a garden where most churches have parking lots. It also has a small, delightful gift shop, Galley West, where handcrafts are sold.

On the Saturday of this wedding, my friend Olive was in charge of the gift shop and expected a quiet morning while everyone enjoyed the gold and blue day. This is her report.

Around nine thirty a young woman rushed in, elegantly dressed but far from serene.

"Oh, please help me," she said. "I am supposed to be at a wedding today but I forgot to bring along my invitation and I don't know which church it is."

"Was it in Orleans?" Olive asked.

"I can't remember. All I know is that it's an Episcopal church. I've been checking every one, from Dennis up."

"This is the right one," said Olive. "I know there's a wedding today because the florists have already been here."

Fortified by a cup of coffee from Olive's coffeepot, the woman hurried out. Before Olive sat down at the desk again, the door burst open to admit a handsome young man in formal attire, ascot and all.

"Do you have any water here?" he asked.

"Oh, yes. I'll bring you a glass."

"I don't exactly need a glass," he said. "The fact is, I'm here to usher for the wedding and I have mustard all over my clothes."

This was quite obvious.

"I stopped for a hot dog," he told Olive. "And it just spilled."

With paper towels and some help, the white shirt came out very well except for a slight dampness. The stain on the trousers would not be noticed.

Quiet returned to the shop, and there was time for Olive to attend to a customer while cars began arriving for the wedding. But at ten minutes of twelve, the phone rang.

"Galley West Gift Shop," Olive said.

"Could you possibly help me?" the voice was tearful. "I have to get a message to the church. It's urgent."

"What is it?"

"It's about the wedding. I'm just leaving Chatham, so I'll be about ten minutes late. I can't find Grandma's flowers. They aren't in the refrigerator."

"Who shall I say called?"

"I'm the bride."

"It was quite a morning," Olive commented. Incidentally, the missing flowers turned out to be in a refrigerator located near the gift shop.

I had thought when my daughter, Connie, was married that everything would be in perfect shape. Certainly I could not have foreseen that the maid of honor would lose one of her contact lenses in the bedroom upstairs. It was finally found under the bed—way under. (At least nobody could have stepped on it while hunting!)

Now it is in fashion to have weddings outdoors, and I admire the courage this takes, especially on the Cape. No weather report can be trusted. The Cape, I think, wants to be independent. But the daughter of a dear friend of ours was determined to have her wedding outdoors near the beach she loves, and for once the fair weather predicted came along. Her father said afterward that although he still felt that weddings belong in churches, the deep blue water and shining sand made a lovely setting.

Standard time begins at the end of this month, and Amber and I face our usual struggle. We have gone along so happily in daylight saving time, and now we have to get used to having everything an hour off. It not only upsets her eating schedule but mine. Amber has a fine time sense. Every morning at ten minutes of nine she gets me up by purring in my ear and patting my cheek. I don't even have to look at the clock. If I happen to get up at seven thirty or eight, she stares at me and switches her tail. Then, at exactly six at night, she shepherds me to the kitchen.

She does not expect time to suddenly juggle the hours. At ten minutes of nine, it is no longer ten minutes of nine: it is now ten minutes of eight, although I am never quite sure of the change until I say "Fall back." I have never really understood why the time change is necessary. I was told years ago that it was to benefit the farmers, but I lived in the country long enough to know that farmers do not wear wristwatches. Their time is set by nature herself. I never can explain to Amber where the missing hour goes because I don't understand it myself. I simply wonder, if I go to bed at midnight, why it is only eleven o'clock by the bedside clock. I have a fantasy that if you collected all the missing hours and added all those gained, they would not come out even. You would find that some rebellious hour had slipped away, and was wandering far out in space upsetting the satellites.

This fall I have had many birds I have not known before, enjoying free meals and good bathing in the birdbath in my yard. At first, I wondered whether I was simply forgetting some former visitors, the way one forgets the name of someone who suddenly turns up after a few years. I was relieved to hear on a news commentary that recent hurricanes had affected the bird migrations, driving many travelers off course with their 150-mile winds. So as I put out more dinners, I am glad to see the newcomers. I hope not too many of our regular birds had already flown south.

I wish my small boarders a safe journey and a safe return when winds are gentle and the earth is green again.

We speak of the past as "the good old days" more than ever lately, it seems to me. In Wisconsin where I grew up, wood for the fireplace came from vast acreages of forest. Father went out for a day with a farmer and his wagon and came back bringing all we needed. Townspeople, of course, had furnaces. The fuel was coal. It had various names according to sizes but all I remember is that it was anthracite. At our house, Papa managed the furnace. He shook the ashes down, stoked at night, shoveled fresh coal in the morning. By and large, the process was simple and the furnace reliable. One time, however, he added a small amount of gasoline when the fire was too low. Fortunately he was a quick jumper and even his reddish curly hair was not singed. Mama's comments were hot enough.

Now with all our modern technology, heating is no longer such a simple matter. Firewood has become a scarce product and a cord may sell on the Cape for $140 (this week). Most furnaces run on oil, the latest luxury item. I am surprised that Neiman-Marcus doesn't display jugs of it along with the sapphires and diamonds.

So last night's supper with my friends Barbara and Slim was a special treat. For I had the experience of dining in a solar house for the first time and of being the guest to christen it.

The entrance leads to the long, spacious living room. The outside wall at the right consists of sliding glass panels from floor to ceiling. They open onto the brick patio, beyond which the pine woods make a green background. At the end of the wall, a door leads to Slim's greenhouse, where, already, plants are growing.

A handsome brick chimney at the end of the room has no big open fireplace but a black iron wood-burning stove, with a pipe opening into the flue. The effect is very handsome, and the stove will provide room heat better than a fireplace.

The long wall opposite the glass sliders has a wide pass-through section in the center. From the small Pullman kitchen, Barbara will not be shut off from the conversation in the living room while she is stirring the creamy chowder.

The living room floor is rosy and bare. This is part of the solar scheme, for the brick is absorbent and takes in the heat and holds it. The kitchen floor has a soft-grey modern floor covering, with a layer of cushioning which saves tired feet. There is only one small, narrow window at the end, for this is not the part of the house that the sun shines on.

Everything in the house is planned to conserve energy and use solar power. Slim and Barbara do have a standby furnace, but expect to use it very little. In their old house, which is next door, the oil bills equaled those of a country inn. And this winter my own small one-story house will run the bill right through the roof. So Slim and Barbara are fortunate pioneers.

What impressed me most was that this new-era house keeps the flavor of the past. No chrome or metal, no tables with pipes for legs. A big comfortable sofa, a drop-leaf table, all wood, all early pine, polished to a soft glow, a big round table such as Grandma had in the parlor. My two favorite chairs are here, moved with the family. One is a black painted rocker with a splint seat (thin woven lengths, not cane or rush but the same material used in pie baskets). The other is a twin of mine at the Connecticut farm. It too is a rocker, a sturdy, low comb-back with a wide seat—made for a substantial sitter. The top is curved the way some combs are. The color of the wood is lighter than most pine or maple. Both chairs suggest hard-working people who sit, oh, so comfortably, and have an afternoon drink while they read a few pages of a book from the wall-to-ceiling bookcase on the inner wall.

Sunlight was spilling on the brick floor as we enjoyed our own drinks. The wall of books added a rainbow of colors to the room, and I decided, as usual, that nothing decorates a home like books. There they are, waiting to decorate the mind, too!

For supper the drop-leaf table is pulled out from the wall. Barbara sets out the same six candlesticks that used to shine over the long table in the formal dining room of the other house. The steaming fish chowder was served in the same old-fashioned, wide, flattish soup bowls, now so difficult to get. As we ate, the sunset glow shone in the sky over the pines. All the way from Rock Harbor across town it came to signal day's end.

I dropped my thoughts in my bag until I got back to Still Cove. Amber gave some suspicious sniffs (You have had that dachshund in your *lap!*) and then went to the kitchen for a snack.

"Amber," I said, "I've been in tomorrow."

I had mourned when Barbara and Slim left the old house, so full of happy memories and so beautiful. My only comment when they told me they were going to build a new, small house, a semi-solar house, was, "Well, you would make a house built of chicken coops fine." Which was not very tactful but expressed my doubts.

But the beauty and peacefulness of the new house had won me over. And even the way of heating it was rooted in the past. In 1690, when my own Stillmeadow was built, central fireplaces provided the heat. Then came stoves, then furnaces, then electric heaters. Now this new home turned again to the sun, which the Indians had also used. We have come full circle.

The end of October finds the Cape tightening up for the winter to come. The second week I may count a dozen boats still anchored in Mill Pond. Then one by one they vanish, hauled away to wait for spring. A boat sitting in a front yard looks so awkward and ungainly! Gardeners begin to wrap hydrangeas and other special bushes in burlap jackets. A tide of mulch rolls over the gardens.

For me, the month's end means that the Lobster Claw closes, and my special haven has its big batten doors barred until another season. The Lobster Claw has brought me many happy hours for many years. It is a large, red, barnlike building that does not overlook the water or have a view of woods. There is no garden, although one year a beautiful poison ivy vine spread glossy emerald leaves on the white fence between the restaurant and the Fish Pool next door. Don Berig, owner of the Claw, discovered it and it went.

Inside, the decor is cheerful and unpretentious. The dining room is not loaded with seascapes or antique spinning wheels. The floor is tile red, polished like a mirror, and the booths are painted what I call sailor blue, glossy and bright. Mary Lou Berig keeps small, fresh bouquets on the tables. One huge, amiable artificial lobster lounges across the left wall; the ceiling is masked with fish net. On the right, casement windows open out to the southwest breeze and the green shadow of locust trees.

But the kitchen is the hub of the wheel in any eating place, and the kitchen at the Lobster Claw is sparkling. This is one of the few restaurants specializing in fish that never smells fishy. The clam chowder, simmering in its twenty-gallon copper kettle, is not potato soup garnished with a few bits of clam. This is the chowder that makes New England famous. The chef's other specialties are just as good: the tender steamers, the savory soft-shelled crabs. If fresh scallops are not available and he has to make do with frozen, the waitresses will mention this to the customers.

Best of all, though, is the atmosphere. Don calls this a family restaurant, meaning that family groups—even those with very young children—are welcome. But it is "family" in other ways as well. For one thing, both Don and his wife work here, helped on weekends by their own two youngsters. Then too, the people who make up the staff care about one another. They all know Bev's six-foot son, Sue's lively kindergartener; they worry about Jimmy's illness and follow the Berig girls' figure-skating careers. They take the same sort of family interest in their regular customers. They have a keen eye for the person who does not look as well as he or she did last Thursday. They suggest an extra cup of coffee, a special dessert. When I turned up for my first lunch there after a stay in the hospital, the entire staff gathered around my table. "We've missed you," Don said, "welcome home."

So it will be lonely when the huge doors are barred. But on April first, the porch will be crowded again with old friends ready to help open up for another season.

This is the time to forget indoor chores and spend every possible moment outside in the crisp bright weather. The way we put it is "plenty of time during the long dark winter."

This is also the time when householders keep the lights on at night, so the roads seem jeweled with gold. The night wind sends more leaves drifting down, and the air smells of autumn. Next month will bring cold rain, maybe snow, and fireplaces glowing on early evenings. But it brings Thanksgiving, too, which is our very special holiday, come down to us from those forefathers who braved the violence of the sea to land in a new world. In spite of everything, we who are here bless them!

November

The eleventh month comes in with the tearing off of a page in the calendar. Nature herself does not usually rip off October overnight. The leaves are down, frost has laid her cold hand on the roses, mist settles over the cranberry bogs. But in sheltered spots some late yellow mums still bloom. Bittersweet berries unfold their orange husks so the inner berries show their vermilion beauty.

My two firethorn, or pyracantha, trees react in different ways to the changing season. The one planted on the right side of the garage looks like an orphan of the storm. The one reaching up to the cricket roof on the opposite side has a fine splash of brilliant orange red. Stu Crosby will get the stepladder and cut me a few branches for a winter bouquet.

Firethorn seems to me like a cross between a tree and a vine. For years I admired my neighbor Orin Tovrov's lavish expanse of it covering the side of his big white barn. Finally I got some of my own. It should always be planted close to a wall or lattice because it climbs. But my best one reached the top of the garage and then sent a tall spire straight up in the air. Perhaps Stu will tether it to the roof, I don't know.

Describing the exact colors of autumn berries, including rose hips, is difficult. Reds shade into orange, vermilion moves toward flame. Not long ago I was discussing this problem with my friend Jan Nelson, who is a gifted artist.

"The English language is too limited," I said. "Not enough color words."

"I don't think so," Jan said. "I never have any trouble."

But she does not need to struggle with language: she expresses color with color itself. Her paintings show intricate variations of every shade on the palette. She could look at the firethorn and make it glow on her canvas. My typewriter puts black words on white paper, which leaves a lot to the reader's imagination!

Last week, Stu pruned the multiflora roses. They remind me of women who are beautiful, bright, and good, but are simply exhausting because they are so clinging. The evergreens at the edge of the water are due to be topped again. They grow so fast that the long curve of the beach is hidden and the view of the opposite shore of Mill Pond is bisected by a cedar tip. Definitely, as we stood in the yard talking, Stu and I were in November. But were we really?

"Do you want more bulbs planted?" he asked.

"I always want more bulbs planted," I said. "Is there any such thing as too many?"

We smiled. We were seeing the bank behind the house starred with white and gold narcissus and ruffled daffodils, and the small glade by the driveway dotted with pink and purple hyacinths.

"I can't move the rose behind the wing until spring," Stu said, thus bringing us back into late autumn where we belonged.

I believe, though, that people who are passionate about flowers can always evoke them in their minds, even in January during a blizzard.

Long cold nights mark November's return, grey rains fall, wind walks in the bronze oak leaves. Over Mill Pond the black-backed sea gulls coast the air, so we know the outer sea is storm-ridden. When the sun does come out, the light is pale gold, the shadows in the piney woods still lie deep. The moon sheds a special grace over the dark water and tawny marshes.

There are many versions of the names Indians gave to the months, but my friend Hal Borland told me long ago that the differences come from the fact that tribes named the moons according to the climate each tribe lived in. So in New England we have a Wolf Moon; the name would not fit the sunny warm land where alligators bask in the Everglades. I do not think anyone yet has compiled a list of all American Indian tribes with the twelve moons of each.

One never-ending discussion on Cape Cod is the arrival of Indian Summer. All fall we have cold spells followed by days as mellow as ripe peaches.

"Isn't this a beautiful Indian Summer day?" I ask Pret, whose house is just up the road from mine.

"I don't know that I'd call this Indian Summer." He adds some vegetable scraps to his compost pile. "No heavy frost yet."

I don't disagree, but I have my own opinion. I think we have bits and pieces of Indian Summer, at various times, from late October to the end of November. In any case, the blessed warmth, lucent skies, blue water, windless air are indeed a spillover from summer. It is time to walk the beach without sand blowing into our eyelashes, time to work in the yard in shirt sleeves, time for afternoon drinks on the patio while the birds splash in the birdbath and make a big to-do over preening. Birds are generally wiser than mankind, so I imagine they are not misled. My mockingbird whisks the last drop from the stone bowl and scolds me. "I was planning on one more bath," he says. Yes, he surely knows.

The first snow inevitably follows a stretch of golden days. The flakes sift from pewter skies in casual circles as if they had no destination. Once, when the granddaughters were small, they ran outdoors to catch handfuls of the starry magic.

"Look, Gram. See what we brought!"

The small delicate palms were dripping by the time the girls reached the kitchen. Solemnly they looked at me.

"They're gone," Alice said.

"We ran as fast as we could," Anne added.

"Yes," I said. "Never mind. I'll always remember that you brought me a handful of snowflakes."

The girls are now tall, slender teenagers, busy with their almost-adult lives. But I remember the snowflakes they tried to bring me on that November day, and the first tentative snowfall still has for me a special magic.

A special treat at Still Cove at any season is an evening of live music when the children get to the Cape for the weekend. Sometimes Alice and Anne play solos or violin-viola duets. Our last recital, however, involved a trio. Three of Alice's friends and their mother were spending a week in Orleans. Alice and Dan had both been at the Downeast Music Center in Maine last summer, while Benjy spent the summer working in New York City to help with college expenses. The boys' sister, Eve, studied in Boston. Now everyone had come for an interlude of Nauset air and Cape Cod sun before the fall schedules began.

Eve is a pianist, but unfortunately we do not have a piano. Alice, however, never parts from her violin except to go to the beach (sand might not improve the tone). Dan had lovingly toted his cello, and Benjy's flute was tucked in his knapsack. So an impromptu trio program was planned.

The three teenagers went into the wing to confer. They are all intensely serious about music. Alice and Dan have already played with youth symphonies at Carnegie Hall and Lincoln Center, Ben has played student recitals at museums and colleges. Now the boys are trying to decide between careers in music or in science. I hope music wins, since both are so gifted. Alice has made her own decision and is enrolled as a freshman at a conservatory.

This was an unexpected occasion, but a few neighbors dropped in and sat at the far end of the living room. Chairs were jockeyed around until there was a semicircle for the players: Dan in the middle with his cello, Benjy at the left with his flute, Alice at the right with her violin. Benjy introduced the program. "We've never played together before as a trio. But we do have some scores with us. So we'll try a few violin-cello-flute pieces for you. Some Mozart, Handel, Corelli. Of course, we'll be mostly sight-reading, but here goes."

It wasn't exactly what one would expect from three in blue jeans, T-shirts, striped sneakers. But when Dan signaled for the first notes, the music cast the spell that only true musicians can create. Even Amber, who had disapproved of all the preliminary furniture-shifting, was enthralled. She perched on an arm of the sofa and never took her eyes off the trio.

The players were relaxed and casual, in spite of their deep involvement in the music. Now and then, as they approached a passage where the tempo was complicated, Dan said softly, "Three—four—five," and once, from the side of his mouth, "Flat." Alice and Ben corrected hastily. Before beginning one especially difficult movement, Dan said reassuringly to Alice, "Now, Ben and I have played this once or twice before. It's sort of rough. You know, fast. Tricky. But if the violin just follows the flute, we'll be OK." It did, and they were.

As the incredible music floated through an open window to Mill Pond, the three young performers were lost in a world of their own. After one especially beautiful movement—slow, lyrical—Danny said, "That was good! Let's play it again."

"Again?" said Alice, flushed with the effort of so much sight-reading. The violin section had been especially challenging.

"Again." Dan was firm. Alice tucked her fiddle back under her chin and smiled.

In the intermission they went to the kitchen and fortified themselves with a light snack of Portuguese bread, assorted cheeses, cold roast beef, turkey, blueberry cake, and a fruit mixture of cantaloupe, grapes, and nectarines, washed down with various cold drinks. Then back to the music again.

They were due to leave the next day but stayed an extra night, going to Helen and Vicky's house since Still Cove was full. This gave the boys a chance to discuss science with Helen and gave their mother and sister a chance for one last walk on the beach. "I haven't been here in fifteen years," their mother said, "but everything's the same. Everything's just as beautiful."

There wasn't time for Dan, captain of his high school tennis team, to play a few games at Eldredge Park with Vicky, who coached the winning team of her school in New Jersey. But perhaps next time.

It was a beautiful visit. And when the next news comes about some teenagers who express themselves by throwing rocks at windows or experimenting with drugs, we will remember Benjy, Dan, and Alice.

Country fireplaces should be cleaned before autumn nights remind us that the long cold is coming. Soot builds up in the chimneys even if careful householders do not burn trash, pine branches, or green wood. City apartment dwellers miss the pleasure of greeting the chimney sweeper. Ours is young, clean-shaven, with bright blue eyes and a merry smile. His machine is the size of a baby whale, and the motor roars into action as Pat manipulates the thick hoses. He crouches on the hearth, head and shoulders up the chimney.

"Sure needs it," he says, pushing his wire brush.

I think of London in Charles Dickens's time. Chimney sweeps wore tall black hats and black suits and, when they climbed to the roof, suggested blackbirds. Then I remember that in Connecticut, at Stillmeadow, our farm friend from across the road would turn up with an armload of heavy chains. He would climb to the roof, agile as a trapeze artist. The lowered lengths of chain swung back and forth, back and forth. Of course, the soot fell to the fireplace black and thick as molasses. And no matter how many old sheets were hung in the opening, the whole room filled with ashes.

"Sure needs it," George always said as he wiped his blackened face.

Now when Pat finishes, he lays clean wood on the hearth. The monster machine rolls out of the house. Pat waves a cheery goodbye.

"Have all the fires you want," he says.

And as the chilly dusk-dark of November moves in, the hearth fire echoes the bright days of summer.

The best gift that visitors from the mainland can bring at this time of year is a load of logs and kindling. Few people here on the Cape are able to cut their own and none of us can get used to the price of "bought wood."

Hardwood makes the best fire, but the time is at hand when we destructive human beings will have burned it all up—it will be an endangered species as man is himself these days. Maple gives a fine warmth; birch is the most beautiful. In my childhood there was all the birch anyone could want, for it is not a long-lived tree and not deeply rooted like the oak and maple. The woods were filled with fallen birches. It was all the rage to strip the bark for craft objects—little birch baskets, tiny canoes, and such. But the craftsmen did not always restrict themselves to bark from fallen trees, and as a result much damage was done. A birch cannot live if it is girdled; the bark is lifegiving.

I did not know the locust tree until I came to Cape Cod. Most of those I see do not have heavy trunks. They are greyish

and knobby looking and lighter in weight than the others. The Crosbys tell me that locust is, nevertheless, a hardwood. I do not argue with the Crosbys, but it does seem more like a softwood; in any case, the quick bright flame makes it a fine starter for a fire, with the big heavy oak and maple to make the fire hold steady.

A birch log is fine to use as a decoration in the fireplace. My dear friend Alice Blinn brought me a truckful from Connecticut when she drove up one summer, and I used to keep two logs on the hearth. I set them aside whenever I was ready to light the fire. The best firewood on the Cape twenty years ago was gathered during long walks on the beach. Driftwood was a ready harvest. It never had sappy pulp, and the salt gave extra color to the leaping flames. Now we can seldom get any: craftsmen prize it for lamp bases, carved ornaments, house decorations of all kinds.

Apple wood is another treasure. If there are any dead apple trees on the Cape (as there must be, for once there were farms here), I have never seen them. The 1938 hurricane took down thirteen in our yard in Connecticut, and we pretended the spicy fragrance of the burning logs was meant to comfort us for the loss of pink and white blossoms in spring and rosy apples in fall.

In all my years with an open fire, I have never had an experience like one I had recently. The fire was laid at the time Nancy and I cleaned the garage—she brought in two armloads of locust. It was warm weather then, so we did not light the fire. We had some long deep rains, but mostly it was muggy, miserable, foggy, but not cold. Then one night I heard a *plop plop* in the fireplace. I decided that raindrops must be falling straight down onto the hearth. The next morning the sun covered Mill Pond with gold and the Canada geese were out. But the *plop plop* kept up. I worried that rain had somehow backed up on the roof and was still dripping in. The following day, when Amber and I were eating breakfast, I put down my coffee cup.

"Amber," I said, "there is someone *living* in the fireplace."

Amber wiped her face with her paw.

"Yes, there is," I told her.

That night, when Olive and Linda came in (they don't drop in, they walk), we sat down and had one of those good conversations possible when you are not at a big party.

In a pause, I decided to tell them something that would only add to the general opinion that I am a bit peculiar.

"Somebody is living in my fireplace," I said.

There was a moment of silence before Olive said, "What makes you think so?"

"It's the sound."

Both of them jumped up and moved across the room. They stood one on each side, looking like those stone pilasters in European cathedrals. They bent over; they turned their heads and stared at each other.

"She's right," said Linda. Her tone implied that it was, nevertheless, impossible.

"They chew," I commented.

Olive had a locust log in her arms, and in the next moment we saw the evidence. They did indeed chew. There were small holes all along the surface of the log. "It's bugs—not carpenter ants, thank heaven, or termites. Bugs."

I felt happy. "For once I am *right!*"

Olive and Linda paid no attention. They were lighting the fire.

I do not like the killing of anything, but the thought of having chewers in my fireplace, day and night, was too much. So now they are gone, and the only sound from the hearth is the soft rustle of the flames and an occasional snap as a branch settles into the glowing coals.

This is the month of the Full Beaver Moon. Once there was a large population of beaver in New England, but this intelligent small animal unfortunately had a rich deep pelt. The lovely pond at our farm in Connecticut was a gift from the beaver, for they dammed up the two woodland streams that flowed down the hill. The farmer across the way told us that when he was a boy, he and his brother used to trap the beaver in our pond. They sold the skins for much-needed cash to put in the cracked teapot on the kitchen shelf.

At least they were not killing just for fun. Nor did they care so much for profit that they exterminated the animal population of that region completely. Other men slaughter hundreds or thousands of innocent animals for those elegant fur coats the beautiful people wear. But after all, killing for profit is perfectly legal. I look at an illustration of a golden woman holding her mink coat open enough to show her diamond necklace. I wonder whether she ever adds up the number of small creatures who screamed as they died. (Or thinks about conditions in the mines where her diamonds were found!)

More and more species are labeled "Endangered," but I am afraid almost all of them are. Perhaps, if we are not careful, man himself will be added to the list. In any case, as I put on my woolen coat, it feels comfortable, and no small ghostly paws clutch at it. Even the "wool" is one of the new synthetic fabrics!

November wind has a sound different from any other. It is easy to imagine the cave of the winds in some mythical Northland where the winds are born and the gods send them out to conquer the quiet air.

But the air itself has a northern chill these days. And it reminds me that, among other things, this is the flu season. In the days when it was called grippe, the explanation of how you caught it was simple. You got chilled going out in a driving cold rain. Or you got your feet wet walking through puddles. In any case, you came down with grippe almost immediately. It was a comfortable theory, but doctors nowadays have discarded it. Grudgingly they do admit, however, that the body loses its resistance when it is exposed to cold and dampness. Then, ah then, the viruses find an open door into the shivering victim and fever, sore throat, chills, coughs, and miseries result.

When grippe was promoted to flu—or influenza—it was taken more seriously. Then we had Russian flu—Swine flu— now we need still another new name. By any name it causes a lot of misery, and most people battle it. I believe a flu inoculation (flu shot) is sensible. So even while I am assuring all my friends that I never catch cold, I turn up at my doctor's just in case. Connie, although she is my daughter, takes a stronger stand. When the first grey winds and chilly fogs begin, Alice and Anne, her own daughters, face the world in knitted caps, woolen scarves, heavy jackets, snug gloves or mittens, warm slacks and socks, and shoes designed for cross-country hiking. A few extra vitamin C's are an added protection. Nevertheless, the girls do succumb to an occasional cold with a cough, I notice, and even flu. Alice specializes in high temperatures, Anne coughs, and Connie settles for laryngitis. With the usual tact of worrying parents and grandparents, I tell her that if only they could move out of the city, they would not be surrounded by viruses.

One thing, the pill parade is a subject of conversation in this weather. The TV commercials suggest that the right pill cures every ailment known to man. Certainly there are enough remedies on the drugstore shelves. Pills come in all shapes, sizes, colors. So do capsules. My friend Barbara and I were discussing medication the other day. She was just recovering from a severe cold and still had several capsules left of her prescription.

"I hate to take them!" she said. "They stick in my throat."

"I've had the same problem," I told her. "I think capsules lurk just far enough down to choke you."

We discussed solutions. Mine, I decided, was a little odd. After choking, re-swallowing, head-tilting, bread chewing, icewater sipping, and so on, I tried using my imagination. I do not look at the capsule and think it is like an orange or blue or green submarine, which might blow up. I try picturing myself lost on a desert. I crawl along the burning sand toward an oasis. At my last gasp, I reach the cool green spot where a spring gushes up under the palm trees. A few gulps of the lifesaving water and the obstruction in my throat is gone, even before I have counted the second camel tilting against the sky. The system would work for anyone. The helping image doesn't have to be located in a desert. A mountain stream, a woodland spring, a lake—any of these would do. The only necessity is feeling such an unendurable thirst that a mouthful of pebbles would be swallowed faster than a champion skier whirls to the finish pole.

Someday I shall find out why capsules are so widely used for medication today. Perhaps they were invented by some man who had a memory of taking castor oil in orange juice when he was a child!

The early snowfalls are not like those that will come later. I do not know why it is so, because the actual temperature varies all during the season, but the powder-fine dry snows come later. The first are clinging and moist, the flakes huge and lacy—each one as big as the white china butter chip I keep on my desk for paper clips. There is usually no wind. The snow settles gently on junipers, cedars, jack pines. My cherished oak has her coppery leaves crested with white. The spread of cranberries on the slope toward Mill Pond looks soft as eiderdown. The stillness is almost tangible.

When I go out to feed the daily gathering of mockingbirds,

cardinals, and chickadees, the snowy yard resembles those scenes on Christmas cards—which should be mailed early, early or they are likely not to arrive until May Day. I am reminded of last season when a holiday note I sent to a friend who lives just around the corner turned up three months later from Wellfleet.

Our own postal workers do the best they can, overworked, underpaid, and operating in quarters about as modern as those in my childhood. They edge their way around stacked cartons, heave bags of mail by hand, cope with postage rates which jump overnight, and, on top of everything else, help confused customers look up zip codes. Rural mail carriers like Bill Ramos, who comes to my house, carry truckloads of mail in small cars and have to wedge into the mailbox mountains of packages, magazines, newspapers, shampoo samples, Postage Due notices, bills, and multiple copies of the same gift catalog—to say nothing of notes from friends and other pieces of what I always think of as "real mail."

"Well, can't last forever," Bill says. "No worse than July and August when the summer people come."

Returned mail is the bane of my own correspondence: I dread those envelopes stamped "Addressee Unknown." When I read the day's mail, except from the family and close friends, I look first for the return address. All too often, it is either missing, illegible, or completely smudged out by long, wavering black lines. The circular postmark may be so dim as to be invisible, but those black lines are clear and distinct. If I am lucky, the correspondent puts name and address inside, but if not, I am lost. Sometimes I try to improvise when I send my reply, guessing at what the correct town must be or omitting an illegible street number. But this does not always work, and back comes my letter. Meanwhile, someone somewhere is saying, "She won't answer her mail."

It might help if the Postmaster General were required to handle his own correspondence from time to time, without any assistance from his staff. Then he might have a clearer picture of the problems that the average citizen has to face. He should look up his own zip codes, struggle to decipher postmarks, remember the constantly rising rates, check the weight of a greeting card accompanied by three snapshots, try to get the stamps to stay on his envelopes without hammering them because they don't have enough glue, and, most of all, keep track of when he has mailed something important and how long it takes to reach its destination.

The big holiday season adds confusion unlimited. Some people I know have decided to give up Christmas cards entirely, but I would miss the annual reunion via the mailbox. Others settle for postals, which are certainly cheaper but too "public," it seems to me, for any really personal messages. We all agree that as soon as the turkey soup is gone, it is time to start mailing.

In fact, my Christmas greetings are piled up on my desk right now, and Amber is pushing them off as fast as she can.

November is a month when the chill blustery days and long cold nights are hard on dieters. Green salads are fine on hot summer days. But the very sound of the wind from the Atlantic against the big window makes me think of a real breakfast of sausage and buttermilk pancakes with first-run golden maple syrup. By suppertime I forget I am a non-dessert-eater, and when I go out to eat, I often order Indian pudding. I have had many very fine puddings, but almost never an authentic Indian pudding. So I like to share the recipe my mother and grandmother used.

Bring 4 cups of milk to a boil in the top of a double boiler. Gently stir in ⅓ cup yellow cornmeal and cook 15 minutes. Add 1 cup dark molasses and remove from heat. Add ¼ cup butter, 1 teaspoon each of salt, cinnamon, and ginger, and ½ cup seedless raisins. Place the batter in a greased baking dish. Then pour 1 cup cold milk over it. Bake in a slow oven for 1½ to 2 hours. Serve with hard sauce or cream or even vanilla ice cream.

The main thing about the real Indian pudding is the cup of cold milk poured over. When I was in college, my room-mate and I used to go into Boston—with special permission from the college—especially to eat at Durgin Park. And the Indian pudding there, as I remember it from those days, was perfect.

Although I grew up in Wisconsin, my parents always consid-ered Massachusetts our real home. When my sister and brother died in infancy, while we were living in Colorado, we brought them back to the family cemetery in West Spring-field to what was called the "final resting place." I was raised as a New Englander, especially as to cuisine. Therefore when I came east to college and had my first Durgin Park Indian pudding, it not only made me homesick but also made me feel at home. The oyster stew, clam chowder, finnan haddie had the same effect. In Wisconsin, we used fresh oysters shipped from Chicago at Christmastime, but the clams were canned and the finnan haddie came in small wooden boxes.

In many countries, people stick pretty much to their own national cuisine. But here in the United States, our dinner table is international. (Perhaps someday we will learn to ap-preciate other attitudes and ways of life as well as different styles of cookery!) I have feasted on southern fried chicken in Virginia and also in Connecticut, and chili, red-eye beans, and tamales in Wisconsin. I tried my first pizza in an Italian café in New York and my first wonton soup at a neighborhood Chinese restaurant in Boston. When I made the traditional trip abroad, I had no trouble enjoying the national dishes in every country. But when I found the Indian pudding at Durgin Park, it was definitely home cooking!

I like to think that on the Cape almost any type of national cooking can be found, from German food at the Inn of the Golden Ox to Polynesian and Chinese at the Double Dragon.

And for those who want "real Cape," there are places like the Eastham Lobster Pool. There you begin with a bucket of soft-shelled clams or oysters on the half-shell. You go on to any Cape fish you desire, lobster, scallops, flounder (or sole, if you prefer), or if you want steak, a perfect steak comes sizzling to the table. For standard New England fare, there is always The Cleaver, with quahaug pie, Caesar salad (don't bring the big bowl or I won't be able to manage anything else, not even steak and stuffed baked potatoes). The Lobster Claw has closed for the season, but those who enjoy dining out will not exactly go hungry.

One special treat is that the Barley Neck Inn has begun serving Sunday brunch. The big mansion has fireplaces in every one of the dining rooms. (Which was once the drawing room, which the library, which a den or study?) The elegant square "lady's grand piano" must mark the music room, except that the polished cast-iron stove is in the same area. At Barley Neck, the Bloody Marys (with or without liquor) come in tall sparkling glasses with a crisp stick of celery for a stirrer. The elegantly printed menu makes it difficult to decide between entrees, except that I myself never have a problem because the eggs Benedict are the best I have ever had anywhere.

Bill, who greets the guests, is also a member of the Orleans baseball team, the Little Necks. I find it hard to imagine him in a baseball uniform! In any case, I often think how much the sea captain who built the mansion would enjoy sitting in the Peach Room by the open fire, trying the rare roast beef or the swordfish.

Whatever the menu, however, we begin to look ahead to the great feast. The main subject of conversation becomes: "What kind of stuffing do you like best for the turkey?" Some of my friends insist on oyster—it gives a delicate, not heavy taste. But chestnut brings a sweet nutty flavor. One friend insists on sausage, another on adding cranberries to the mixture. I think most of the recipes are interesting, but I choose the regular old-fashioned turkey stuffing. This is because I think the main business of stuffing is to absorb the essence of the beautiful bird itself and, when served, to be receptive to giblet gravy (the main reason for turkey in the first place).

The story of the first Thanksgiving does not arouse much interest nowadays, it seems to me. Except, perhaps, among schoolchildren. Thinking back to when my own daughter was an earnest little Pilgrim in the school pageant, I can still hear that piping voice practicing her recitation over and over:

"In sixteen hundred and twenty
On a rough and barren coast
The Pil'rims started a 'settle-mint'
And established a trading post."

And I can still remember the despair that swept through the entire family on the morning of the great performance when we discovered that there wasn't a single large-sized safety pin anywhere in the house and that the waistband of my black crepe skirt, the most essential item in her costume, couldn't be fastened snugly in any other way. I can't remember how we solved the problem. I suspect that her teacher, being an old hand at school productions, had an emergency kit full of safety pins and sewing supplies.

When my granddaughters reached that age, Alice, too, was a Pilgrim in white paper collar and cuffs, while Anne was lucky enough to be a Wampanoag squaw and got to paint her face with red and yellow streaks.

However, except in the schools, the story of the first Thanksgiving seems to be taken pretty much for granted. Of course, the churches will be bright with autumn foliage and glowing displays of seasonal fruits and vegetables, and the service will center on our gratitude for all that God has given us during the past year and our need to share our bounty with those who are less fortunate. And when the whole family gathers around the dinner table, we will feel, as always, a special thankfulness that we can all be together once again.

But what will we talk about? An unusual recipe for pumpkin pie, a football game, a piece of family news, the latest headlines? How many of us will even think of the old story that explains how this celebration of Thanksgiving first began?

I have just been reading a book based on William Bradford's own account, and I am surprised to find out how little I know about the original holiday. The Pilgrims were not celebrating a very good harvest, it turns out. Their twenty acres of corn had done well (thanks to Squanto), but their six or seven acres of English crops—peas, barley, wheat— had failed. Bradford comments cautiously that this was due either to "ye badnes of ye seed, or latenes of ye season, or both, or some other defecte." All the same, they were able to increase the weekly food ration a little: in addition to one peck of meal per person (from the *Mayflower*'s supplies), they now received one peck of maize. Eleven buildings had been finished, relations with the Indians were peaceful, and there had been no illness for some months. All this was reason enough to declare a holiday so that, as Bradford puts it, they might "after a more special manner, rejoyce together."

So they set the date—it was in October—and sent an invitation to Massasoit. They were somewhat dismayed when he turned up with ninety braves, but the great chief dispatched several hunters into the forest and before long was able to contribute five deer to the feast. (It is a welcome guest who brings a gift of food!) In addition, the menu included roast goose, roast duck, eels, clams, and other shellfish, two kinds of bread—white and corn—and bowls of crisp watercress, leeks, and other "sallet greens," all washed down with wine, white and red, made from wild grapes and "very sweete & strong." There is no record that the Pilgrims ate any of the wild turkeys they saw running in the woods or the cranberries that filled nearby bogs. Neither is there any mention of pumpkin pie: for dessert they had wild plums and dried berries.

All in all, it was a fine holiday. The feasting went on for three days, Captain Miles Standish staged a parade, both Pilgrims and Indians played games of skill and chance, and there was probably plenty of singing and dancing. The celebration was such a success, in fact, that it was repeated every year. But it was not until 1863, in the middle of the Civil War, that Abraham Lincoln proclaimed it a national holiday and set aside the date in November.

The first Thanksgiving was hardly over, however, when the Pilgrims discovered that they had grossly overestimated their harvest. The meager weekly ration had to be cut in half, and people braced themselves for another grueling winter. Still, they did not lose hope; with God's help, they would survive.

The lesson is worth remembering, I think. Especially when life seems grim, it is good to be reminded of those early New Englanders: of their courage and fortitude—and their faith.

And so the cherished holiday is here again, with the traditional turkey and giblet gravy, snowy mashed potatoes, tender-sweet turnips, golden squash, and pumpkin pie. In the country, children roast chestnuts over the hearth fire. In the city, street vendors pop the shiny brown nuts over braziers. When day is done, parents and grandparents reminisce, happy over shared memories. Children have a way of idling into the kitchen because cold turkey has a special charm. And the puppy and kitten are already at the refrigerator door.

"Turkey is my favorite food of all," one of the grandchildren says dreamily. "That and lobster."

And it occurs to me that courage takes many forms. Crossing the sea calls for one sort—it is heroic and we remember it. But who was the man who first dared toss a lobster on a bed of coals and discover the delicate pink-white richness inside?

The *Farmer's Almanac* reminds me that November is the next-to-last month. It is time for long thoughts about the ten months now to be folded away in memory. It is better to list the shining hours and erase the dark ones. Add up sunsets at Rock Harbor with children silhouetted against the apricot sky as they run free, free, free. Or the emerald of the summer marshes; the wild roses starring hillsides above the sapphire water; the early morning birdsongs, tuning up like some miniature symphony.

Late autumn is far from dreary for winter residents on the Cape. Summer people find this hard to believe. No swimming, no beach parties, no tennis or sailing, no summer theater or Melody Tent. Who wants to go ice fishing? They think of the Cape only as a summer resort. Which is probably just as well, for the fifteen Cape towns need the autumn and winter and early spring to live a quieter life, repair summer damages, and get ready for the time when, once again, the wind blows soft along the bridge that leads to this land set in the frame of infinite blue waters.

Meanwhile, Thanksgiving is a blessed holiday.

December

This morning I crept out of bed at dawn to turn the furnace up a notch. The Atlantic winter winds are not defeated by insulation, storm windows, or a sturdy roof. When I looked out, the whole sky was apricot; Mill Pond, too, shimmered with apricot. There was still no sign of the sun, but its presence was there. Somehow the vast unity of color made the immensity of sky deeper and wider than the whole universe, and the sea, a spillover of more sky. As the comforting hum of the furnace rose, I stood marveling. Why are no two sunrises ever the same? Why does nature give us a lifetime of sunrises with every one astonishing?

Why are sunsets, too, always unique? When we go to Rock Harbor to watch the great, blazing orb sink into the sea, why do the colors never repeat? Even in midwinter, children race on the icy sand while parents sit in cars with the heaters on, watching spellbound as the flaming sky fades into darkness.

One day last summer, Olive and I drove down to the harbor and parked near a car with out-of-state license plates. We could hear the couple inside talking about business, dates, finances. But as the final plunge of the sun began, they were silent. Then the man spoke.

"That's one thing they can't commercialize—sunset!" he said. Which summed it up pretty well.

I hear from inlanders a constant refrain.

"We want a place on Cape Cod. On the water, of course!"

This reminds me that although you can still find properties on the water if you are very lucky and very determined—they are scarcer than roses in January—nobody can ever have both sunrise and sunset as their main attraction. If you live on the ocean side of the Cape, sunrise dazzles your eyes, but if you are on the bay side, you watch incandescent water ripple at the edge of twilight.

Life, after all, is a succession of choices. As far as this one goes, I am living on the wrong side, here where the main windows all face east. For I am a night person. So is my cat. If we do manage to greet the dawn, we are back in bed before the electric blanket has cooled down. But for sunsets, we drive across to the other side of town to Rock Harbor. We choose the golden light that comes at day's end when we are as lively as the four crickets singing away in the house. One special blessing of Cape Cod is that you are never far from one shore or the other.

Days are shorter now—a much briefer span of full daylight, together with, as Hal Borland used to say, "a few minutes at each end to turn the lights on." But this is the way it has always been: we expect it, nothing to worry about. The Full Cold Moon comes, and the still beauty of the night deepens when a solitary owl hoots in the woods. The melancholy call is another reminder that nature's rhythm is changeless, even in this changing modern world.

The falling snow, coming just when the *Almanac* predicted it would, is part of the age-old pattern of the seasons too. The only problem is, "Where did we leave the snow shovel? Look behind the beach umbrella!"

In December the moon has a silvery glow, which Mill Pond echoes. The winter stars have a clarity that brings them close. I think this is because the icy winter air lacks the haze of warmer seasons.

In the early morning, Mill Pond has a polished look. If there are clouds in the sky as the sun rises, the color is dazzling. The clouds spread a blue-grey shadow across the water. Spaces in between catch the clear pink of the rising sun. This is a time to wonder at the miracle of nature. Night follows day, spring follows winter—mankind may pursue the path of destruction, but the tide rises and falls in its usual pattern. Sometimes it covers the landing strip on Mill Pond, and that makes conversation in the neighborhood. But we are not frightened, because we are sure the tide will recede.

This is also the season for thinking about gifts: making them, hunting for them in the shops, buying, giving—and receiving. I believe the best gift Cape Cod gives the city people who come here in the summer is the chance to be close to nature. There is sand to walk on or green grass dotted with buttercups or dandelions. There is clean, clean air, sweet with pine and honeysuckle. The eternity of the sea has not yet been diminished by wars. The piney woods flicker with bird wings. Sometimes a deer leaves hoofprints by a small pool.

To be sure, the gift shops are exciting, with their beach plum jelly, cranberry relish, shell jewelry, paintings of Rock Harbor. But the memories of days on the beach are even better. Those of us who do not have to leave can only hope that a gift of serenity was tucked into each of the cars crossing the bridge to the mainland.

And now we who remain here can look up at the quiet winter sky and feel restored. May peace be with us all.

As I skimmed ice from the birdbath this morning, I thought how much we take for granted. Ice is right at hand all year round. We open the refrigerator door, pull out a plastic tray, and there is the ice. For a big party, we pop downtown and stop by a metal machine, feed it a coin, and drive off with a plastic bag full of neat cubes. To keep foods fresh, we have freezers, freezing compartments in refrigerators, refrigerated trucks, and so on. None of this seems at all remarkable.

But not so long ago, ponds and lakes were watched anxiously in late fall and early winter until the ice was thick enough to be harvested. Cutting out the huge blocks, sawing them, dragging them to shore, hauling them to the icehouse was one of the hardest jobs men had. The icehouse was windowless, and as the cakes were hoisted in, sawdust buried them. The following summer, the 50- or 100-pound cakes were dug out as needed to keep milk, butter, eggs safe. People who did not have their own icehouse waited for the ice wagon to make its rounds. The hefty chunk that was deposited in the ice chest on the back porch then had to be hacked up with an ice pick so that the icebox in the kitchen or pantry could be filled. Every so often the child whose daily chore it was to empty the drop pan under the icebox forgot the job, and then mopping a flooded floor was another part of the ice routine.

In an old house on the Cape I saw one early icebox that was simply a sea chest with a lead box in one end for the ice. There was a hole in the bottom of the chest and a pan on the floor underneath to catch the melt. I remembered suddenly that in addition to the danger of flooding there was another problem with the old-fashioned iceboxes. The flat top of the ice cake was fine for a small plate of butter or a piece of pie. But sometimes the dishes melted the ice and then slid easily down small rivers to the bottom of the box. Mince pie and beef stew never made a happy match.

My grandfather's farm in West Springfield had a fine kettle-hole sweet-water pond, and the icehouse stood at the edge. It was off limits to children, but my cousins and I spent a good many afternoons there all the same, sliding around in the cool damp sawdust and digging down to the buried treasure. The boys chipped long slivers of frozen crystal for us. The secrecy added a special savor!

As I turned toward the house, I reflected that although ice is not usually thought of as a gourmet treat, the taste of ice from a pure spring-fed pond is completely unlike the modern product, just as those tiny wild strawberries are unlike the plump domestic variety. The old way of getting ice was inconvenient, but it did have advantages.

Back in the kitchen, Nancy was filling the dishwasher with all the glasses and silverware from the cupboard. They would be ready in no time for the holiday season. No heating water in the kettle and swishing soap flakes in the enamel dishpan. No dousing with a scalding rinse and polishing with red-checked dish towels. No rubbing of forks with Wright's silver cream. The old hand methods were more personal, but the new ways are certainly faster. In five minutes, Nancy had joined me by the fire for some of the apple cake Millie sent over yesterday.

Speaking of clean dishes reminds me that Moondust, my skunk, sleeps through the cold spells but someone else always licks the dish clean. Could it be raccoons? In any case, anything that is put out vanishes like dew in summer. Recently, Nancy and I emptied on the frozen ground an entire cupboardful of stale crackers, cookies, cornmeal, flour, and cereal. The banquet resulted from my first experience with those small mothlike creatures that *take over* the kitchen. (In this case, it was my kitchen.)

While Nancy tossed everything by the fence, we discussed various theories about these annoying little bugs. Sometimes they arrive in bags of flour from a supermarket. Sometimes they move into cracker boxes through infinitesimal holes. We discovered an added fact—they begin as worms! One box of cornmeal was full, but of worms—the cornmeal was packed inside them. Nancy remarked that it showed how long it was since I made cornmeal muffins.

When we sat down for tea, I remembered the one time before that I had seen these invaders. It was in the kitchen of an elegant mansion owned by the editor of a magazine I worked for. I was in that dream kitchen because I was writing copy about the remodeling job just completed.

Such a kitchen! Buckingham Palace could not be so perfect. As I walked around filling my yellow pad with enthusiasm, I stopped in front of a counter which had six canisters lined up at the back. They were decorated with flower paintings. What possessed me to open the biggest one, I have no idea. It was labeled "Flour," and flour was what it held. But the flour was jumping up and down! I was still standing there staring when my boss came in.

Life is full of crises, and at that moment, this seemed to be a major one. Should I report the infested flour to my superior, who would undoubtedly tell the editor's wife? But what then? The cook might be dismissed or she might depart on her own, once she sampled the temper of her employer. Then too, Miss Blinn, my boss, was my idol. She had had an exhausting day, full of problems. How would she feel about having that flour container dumped in her lap, so to speak? But suppose I reported directly to the owner of the house? I would not have my name on the list of staff members of the magazine much longer, that was certain. She was a perfectionist. She would hardly be pleased to have it get around—and such things always do—that her elegant kitchen was infested with bugs.

Personally, I did not want my career to be snuffed out by a can of worms. I had a family to support. What did I do? I snapped the lid back on that canister so fast it banged.

"It's the most beautiful kitchen I ever saw," I said.

"I liked the Lunts' better," Miss B commented.

It is strange how memories return. I thought I had forgotten how guilty I felt at the thought of the hostess and guests reaching out to a silver platter for one more light roll! For if the cook needed new glasses, she might not have noticed that the flour was jumping.

When Nancy brought more tea, I finished my thoughts. Most homemakers feel that a clean kitchen has top priority above all else. In cities like Manhattan, they must get used to the constant battle with cockroaches, because the whole magic city is underlined with them and they invade like armies. When I met my first one, I almost fainted. And I never outgrew my conviction that if my kitchen were really clean, they would go away. Somehow, it had to be my fault. Now, years later, I felt the same emotion.

These recent invaders were discovered in midwinter, but they could have been found at any time of year, I think. There are plenty of seasonal pests as well. Here on the Cape we have ants—carpenter ants and small russet-colored ones which build sand pyramids in the yard and then leave them to move into the house. We have spiders—last summer broke all records. Ticks are a major problem, especially for pet owners. And we have wasps! Their convention hall at Still Cove is the bird feeder, where they carpet the roof and the orange halves. It is only possible to replace the dried shells with juicy new ones in the pitch black. The wasps go to bed somewhere else.

On a hot afternoon, flies are everywhere, especially if the door is held open fifteen minutes while someone is saying, "No, I can't stop in." The greenheads are the worst. We spend a lot of time discussing the sure-cure lotion, salve, Rx for that itching poison. But we accept these plagues. It is only when we face enemies inside cracker boxes or bags of flour and cornmeal that we really object, for then it is our deep pride which is damaged.

In any case, a feast of saltines and suchlike went out to the yard. By morning the next day, there was not a crumb left. I couldn't help wondering who ate the bugs and whether the mockingbird liked the hoecakes sent me from Virginia.

Yesterday morning, I found that a fresh dusting of snow had fallen. The air was full of birds, and Tiny Tim skipped along the split-rail fence. I didn't notice the debris in the yard because I was dazzled by four cardinals swooping in to the bird feeder. Against the whiteness of the snow, they blazed with scarlet. This winter I am sure they are bigger than usual, and certainly they are more confident. They even face the blue jays with bravery. I sometimes have wondered whether the dominant flame of their wings is a gift from nature to reassure them, just as a timid young girl finds confidence in a new and expensive dress.

As I stood watching them, I thought of Robert Frost's little poem about how a discouraging day was saved for him when a crow, perched in a hemlock, shook down a dust of snow. For me, it was a flash of cardinals.

A good snow gives the earth a comfortable blanket, better than the fallen leaves. At our Connecticut farm it sometimes blanketed the old house so far up the windows that the downstairs wore a grey twilight. When we could not open a single outside door, we did not appreciate that blanket. Shoveling kept the whole family limp. So it has always pleased me that the Cape has less snow. When it comes, though, it is so beautiful it leaves me breathless. The evergreens were meant to cradle the white flakes. The woods frame Mill Pond, and the cold sky above and the icy water below take on an extra glitter.

When the temperature rises, the eelers come by in small swift boats. They usually anchor where the little duck pond opens into the bigger water. When Amber and I get up in the morning we watch them. One boat has two figures standing, one in bow, one at stern. They wear, bless them, scarlet, electric blue, green garments, as if they meant to be a dramatic focus. They hold what look like long poles and bend to draw something up, then stand upright again.

I wish them luck because when I used to fish for flounder there, I brought up a long swiveling eel much too often.

An eel in a canoe is no treat. I cut the line and felt miserable the rest of the day at dealing out death in this shoddy manner.

I know eels are delicious eating, a special delicacy in elegant cuisine. In fact, one summer when Jill's son, David, and his wife, Anne, together with their children and golden retriever, spent their vacation on Snow Shore Road, David had a fine time eeling, and Anne loved the catch. I discovered it when I went over for a clam and broiled flounder dinner. I walked across the back yard to the back door. The clothesline was stretched between two locusts, and over it hung three eels. They looked like lengthy snakes to me, and I was glad Anne did not feature them for dinner. A bucket of Little Necks was fine!

When Jill's daughter spent her honeymoon in our cottage, Barbara found out that Val thought eels were the best delicacy the sea provided. When he made a catch, they solved the first hurdle in matrimony, for Val cooked and ate his eels alone outside the house. Barbara did not even look from the window.

"Darling," Val said, "they were delicious! I'm sorry you missed them."

Eating habits seem about as personal as haircuts for men or makeup for women. But background has a great deal to do with it. Could anything compare, for instance, with Grandmother Raybold's Plum Pudding? National and regional cookery appeals to the people who grow up with it in their home ground. But in this era countless human beings are uprooted and live half a world away from their native country. One way to assuage homesickness is to keep the eating habits. So now the current cookbooks specialize in Chinese, Italian, French, Spanish, Japanese, Hawaiian, even English. (The discovery that English cookery produces some delectable dishes is long overdue.)

Today in our country Julia Child must be the universal guide to cookery. But she began by studying in France, and her early television shows were all about the art of French cooking. She now includes a variety of gourmet dishes, which I think is a fine idea.

I am biased because of my own experience. Dione Lucas, the famous French expert, once came to Waterbury, Connecticut, to give a year's course in French cooking. Class was held in an auditorium with the stage set with cooking equipment, a stove, a worktable. I do not remember an electric refrigerator, and this was long before electric skillets or deep fryers.

At that time I was cooking for five people in our 1690 farmhouse in a real country area (our best friend milked his cows in the big barn just down the road). I had the old milk room in our house for a refrigerator, but the cast-iron range in the back kitchen was where the turkeys roasted, hams baked, stews simmered. I did traditional New England cooking with pure Massachusetts flavor, just as my mother used to do. Why I decided it would benefit the family if I took a course in French cooking is one of those mysteries my life is full of.

I wore my good suit and silk blouse the day I tiptoed into the auditorium and sat in a back seat. This was a bad beginning, because I could not see all the elegant kitchen utensils hung over the work area. The place was packed with stylish young women who looked as if they would be more at home at a country club.

Dione Lucas glided onto the stage and waited for the applause to die down. She was Paris from her high heels to her cap of sleek black hair. Her dress that day was a simple dark-red sheath. Her narrow high-boned face with dark bright eyes had elegance in every eyelash. (When I see the ample figure of Julia Child and her comfortable easy face, I feel sure I am imagining Dione Lucas!)

She began to lecture in a clear rhythmical voice, the French accent bubbling through it.

She knew the culinary art down to the last mushroom sau-téed and added to the wine sauce. Her hands swooped back and forth among dozens of utensils, most of which I had never seen before. The three sizes of French whisks fascinated me, and so did a copper omelet pan. As she demonstrated the recipes, we copied them down in our notebooks. (Mine, unfortunately, is lost.) When the session was over, I drove back to the farm in time to get supper. Four or five cockers met me at the gate as usual. Two Irish setters raced up from the pond where they were helping Jill, my housemate, check on the muskrat holes in the banks. Seven barn cats from the farm across the road were already by the back door. The Siamese and Manx greeted me when I went into the kitchen.

I stood and looked around. There was a big old hot-water radiator under the window. Jill made a long narrow wooden box to cover the top and provide enough space for storage of our kitchen knives, spoons, forks, tea strainers, graters, and so forth. I stared at the collection with new eyes.

"There isn't one French whisk," I told the Siamese. "No Mouli grater. No steel slicer."

The gleaming copper pans that decorated the stage did not belong here. A cast-iron frying pan, an iron Dutch oven, and a few aluminum pans equipped my country kitchen.

As I began to slice cucumbers and tomatoes for the salad, I realized I would never have time to cook any of those marvelous French dishes Dione Lucas spoke about. Saturday night at our house would be baked beans and brown bread as usual.

Nevertheless, I kept on with the Dione Lucas lessons and enjoyed imagining the glamorous world in which five- or six-course dinners were customary.

And anyone can dream of a Lucas or Julia Child dinner while driving one child to kindergarten, picking up another at the ball field, taking a third for the music lesson two hours later, shopping at the supermarket, being home long enough to put a load of laundry in the washing machine, and, if lucky, getting into the kitchen in time to cook fresh peas (instead of frozen), get pork chops baking with sauerkraut, and toss a salad. No time for a chocolate mousse with whipped cream topping: dessert will be fruit.

The solution, I think, would be to set aside one whole day a week—or one in two weeks—shut yourself in the kitchen and *cook, cook,* all day long.

Cooking is fun, especially in winter!

I must admit that there is apt to be a lag in meals between Thanksgiving and Christmas. It is such a busy time—the busiest of the year. So I was pleased to hear the local radio station announce that Ellis's Market was advertising Rock Cornish game hens. They are delicious enough for a company dinner but very simple to cook.

This is another link with the past for me, because the first time I heard of these birds was when Victor Borge, the fabulous Danish pianist, bought some farmland outside our town of Southbury and made his home base there. He raised Rock Cornish game hens. When he was not on tour or flying to Europe to get some sort of award, he lived on his farm. Perhaps he would not be flattered to know I always connect him with his game birds!

An easy recipe for them calls for 2 small game hens, fresh or frozen, cleaned. Heat 3 tablespoons butter and 3 tablespoons olive oil in a heavy pan. Brown the hens in this, turning to brown evenly. Add 2 cups white table wine, and seasoned salt and pepper to taste. Cover and cook for about 20 minutes (if they are frozen, cook until tender when pierced with a fork). Then add 6 chopped shallots (or green onion tops) and 2 cups button mushrooms. Cook 20 minutes longer. Lay the birds on a hot platter and pour the sauce over. Serves 4 to 6.

I like this served with fluffy rice and a salad. I have two more elaborate recipes for game hens, but this one leaves time to wrap a few more Christmas presents.

The wrapping is a wonderfully satisfying job, especially if you have as your assistant a puppy or two or an intently watching cat. But the shopping that comes before it is another matter. The Christmas spirit seems far away when we are caught in a last-minute rush, with its traffic jams and aching feet and that awful moment when we discover, late at night, that we still have six presents to wrap and *no* more Scotch tape anywhere in the house.

A few well-organized people avoid all this by planning ahead, but most of us are caught, year after year. But then as we tie a red bow around the jar of spicy cranberry relish that was simmered in our own kitchen last fall, we suddenly imagine the smile that will light the face of the receiver (who lives in the city and does not make homemade preserves), and somehow, we begin to feel in a Christmas mood after all. And when we open the package from the youngest members of the family and take out the lovingly woven potholder (made last Halloween, judging from the orange and black colors), the slightly lopsided clay dish ("For pepper clips," says the card), and the rather wizened pomander ball (made with a lemon, as we have heard from adult sources, because doing an orange turned out to be too hard—poking in all those cloves can take forever), the day seems truly festive.

Then we remember the Christmas when everybody in the family got the idea of giving scented soap to everybody else. We must have had the cleanest household in town. And the time I received *three* copies of the same new book on the Brontës that I myself had given to two other people. Remembering, we realize that the old cliché is true: it really is the thought that counts.

This year, the fireplace at Helen and Vicky's house will have a new stocking hung up at the corner. For a new youngster has come to live at Holly Hill. Her full name is Hollyberry Red Arrow, and she is an eleven-week-old Irish setter. She is small—a cozy armful of warm, satiny fur, wagging tail, lapping tongue—and she greets every morning as if it were Christmas morning. Her picture stands on my table next to a picture of my own Holly at that age—we speak of them as Holly One and Holly Two—and every time she comes here for a visit, it is a celebration.

December is a good month for parties anyway. Summer involves so much meeting of planes, taking people to planes, "showing the Cape to Aunt Mary, who has never been outside Montana before"—and so on. But now we see our neighbors in our homes instead of at the meat counter at Ellis's. The party may be nothing more complicated than having a few friends over for a simple casserole or even just a drink in front of the fire. But with an open blaze on the hearth or a glossy cast-iron stove radiating cheerful warmth, the occasion is festive enough. Candles add the final touch.

And then popcorn, crisp and buttery. Chestnuts roasted over the embers are as delicious now as in Charles Dickens's time. And, of course, best of all is good talk. When we visit with our friends these days, we try to keep the conversation relaxing. We have agreed that November was a terrible month—and we don't add up the reasons. We talk about the whales off Provincetown but not about the fight against illegal whaling. We discuss whether the tree Jerry Evans planted in the middle of the parking lot can possibly live, with only the small square of real earth around it. We shall be watching it next spring so eagerly.

We carefully keep off the agenda any mention of the offshore oil drilling at George's Bank, but we do wonder if there will really be a floating pier off Snow Shore. The wildlife in our neighborhood is a never-failing topic. Why do the stray cats tiptoe around on the hood of my car every night? The roof too has delicate paw marks. Why do the night people dig up those spring bulbs and then just lay them down? How many Canada geese are still in the little duck pond? Garden talk never lags, either. Houseplants are unpredictable. The one thing we agree on is that no two are alike, no matter what the species is.

It is not that we are closing our eyes to all the problems around us. It is just that a winter evening in front of the fire is a relaxed and peaceful time.

The birds that are permanent residents here at Still Cove live pretty well in winter. The whole front yard is their feeding station. The birdbath and feeder are right beside the split-rail fence which is so comfortable to perch on. Outside the fence, the junipers and cedars and one pear tree make a good shelter from the storms. The branches also arch over the paw-made path that leads to the burrow of my first skunk, Blackberry. Now Moondust has opened it up again.

Strangers might find the scene not exactly suitable for *House Beautiful*. The roof of the bird feeder is usually adorned with two orange halves or a grapefruit half, firmly impaled on nails. Another half is spiked on top of a nearby fencepost. Both the cardinals and Tiny Tim like citrus fruit. A sizable space of lawn is shoveled clear of snow and is deep with cracked corn and mixed birdseed for the ground feeders. The twenty-two quail scurry in on schedule. Nearby, a fire-red dog dish holds drinking water for canine visitors and also supplements the supply in the birds' own birdbath.

A battered white enamel dish is filled with leftovers, some of which are picked over by choosy eaters and then dropped on the ground. At least, the Still Cove yard is a sociable place! My friend Linda, who can see a glint of humor in

almost anything, says kindly, "You could call it picturesque."

The trees, at least, look just as they should, standing quiet and strong in the softly falling snow. The evergreen belongs to December. Experts say that pines are 50 to 100 million years old, which means they preceded us on the earth. For early man, they represented continuity: spring, summer, fall, winter, they were forever green—the color of life.

Today, spruce, pine, hemlock all come indoors to join our Christmas celebration. And of course we deck the halls with boughs of holly and hang up the mistletoe with its waxy white berries and soft blue-grey leaves. We gather ground pine and partridgeberry for the mantel and cut branches of pine for winter bouquets. The juniper is my favorite because of the plump, silvery berries. I imagine that they grow in thicker clusters here on the Cape than on the mainland, but then, I am not impartial.

I have my own theory that the amazing sand that supports the Cape is full of magic ingredients from the glaciers, which crushed mammoth rocks as they moved down from the North. Gardeners must add various supplements to feed the shrubs in their gardens, but the untouched woods around Still Cove are flourishing. They are so thick only rabbits, raccoons, skunks, and possums can squeeze through them. In the years I have been here, our junipers have grown until stars could catch in their tips.

The giant blue boulder which is just below the picture window is visible if I peer through a space cut out between two robust pines. How I wish my father could see it! His magnifying glass would go over every inch of the boulder. Then he would tell me where the granite came from, judging by its composition. The scratches along one side (they are called striations, I think) show the direction of travel. Now a crack has opened at the top, and ice freezes in it every winter. I suppose in a few hundred or thousand years, the whole rock will split. And how long will it be before the sand on that particular stretch of beach will sparkle with flecks of blue?

I have a belief that even long after my boulder has become sand, the pines will still be reaching toward the sky! So as I fill the quail pitcher with juniper, I feel a sense of security. Part of our universe will go on, part will endure. The pines are a kind of promise.

I do not know when the first Christmas tree was chosen for the ritual celebrating the birth of Jesus. My own memories go back to childhood in Wisconsin, when my father went to the big woods and brought back a tree so big that it would not go in the front door. Whatever he did, he did in a big way. He always chose a blue spruce, and it was many years before I discovered that a Christmas tree did not have to be blue spruce. Nowadays, spruce is scarce and has become the tree favored on tree farms.

At Stillmeadow, in the Connecticut valley, we set out a whole slope above the swamp with tiny spruce. Someday, we said, we will be able to go out and cut our own Christmas tree. But every year we decided that the trees were still too small and went to buy one ready cut, unless, of course, the children happened to find a suitable cedar in the woods. The year when our planted trees were finally tall enough to cut, strangers came by in the night and took almost all of them. Just how anyone knew that on our quiet rural acreage there was a stand of fine blue spruce, we never found out. The few trees that are left are like a calendar, marking the years of growth.

One hopeful note is that now many people buy live Christmas trees planted in wooden tubs. These can stay in the house for four or five days and then should go outside, roots wrapped snugly in heavy burlap. In a sheltered place, they have a good chance of surviving. Last year, Olive plowed through the snow at dawn on Christmas Day and set in my yard a small live blue spruce, festooned with strings of cranberries and popcorn. When Amber and I got up for breakfast, the blue jays and chickadees were already investigating the holiday treats. I have never seen a lovelier, merrier tree.

The little blue spruce now grows happily on the slope above the house. It makes me wish that for every Christmas tree cut down and destined eventually for the dump, a healthy young seedling were planted. This would be a new tradition worth cultivating!

The old traditions in our family came with us from Connecticut to the Cape. As always, we take down the huge box of ornaments from the top shelf—not one of those practical new cardboard chests, with dividers to separate the fragile objects as neatly as eggs in a carton, but the same old grocery box we have always used—and carefully unwrap the precious collection. The three-legged lamb is there, and the glass icicles with no tips, and the little angel who has to balance against a twig because she has only one wing. (Over the years a succession of puppies and kittens have tried to use the ornaments as toys.)

And, of course, there are the quaint cookie-dough wreaths and birds that the grandchildren used to make when they were small. The tree would be incomplete without these well-loved treasures. But in addition, there are newer items: a delicate macrame snowflake that a friend wove for me, several elegant seashells with tiny, glued-on hooks, and three pale sand dollars, whose delicately traced star pattern is the perfect Christmas symbol.

I always think of my dear friend Faith Baldwin when it is time to set up the Christmas tree, for trimming it was a special ceremony with her. Long after the four children could not get back home for Christmas, she had a tall tree brought in. The tip touched the ceiling and the branches spread wide. Piles of boxes filled one end of the room. She unpacked the ornaments and decorated the tree herself. She associated the special ornaments with certain friends and sent loving thoughts to them as she worked. And it *was* work for her since the tree was big and she was little: eighty-three pounds was her usual weight. Her silent prayer was for love to replace hate. Faithie is gone now, but as I unwrap the ornaments for our own tree, I think of her and echo her prayer.

Here in Orleans, the custom has always been to tie pine branches to the telephone poles. I had never seen this before. But everyone's favorite is the life-size crêche in the ancient cemetery which fronts on Main Street. Somebody once suggested moving the crêche to the little park near the library, but I never heard any praise of this.

"Let's keep it where it belongs," was the common objection.

Christmas lights festoon trees and bushes outside many houses. The quiet winter nights glow with holiday colors. The times in our remembrance when the lights were out were dismal. Blacked-out windows were bad enough, but holidays should be shining! If we look ahead to another time of deprivation, I would suggest doing without any extra use of electric power all year long, but saving for the green, scarlet, gold of those Christmas lights.

And when the falling snowflakes star the pine branches, the Cape is decorated by nature. Christmas is coming to bless us.

Christmas Eve in our family means reading aloud Dickens's *Christmas Carol*. The Yule log burns and candles flicker on the harvest table. Bowls of nuts and apples, crackers and cheese are within reach of almost every chair. "Just to keep the wolf from the door," said my granddaughter Alice, when she was ten. "Listen," said her younger sister, Anne, "any wolf that came to this house would get a handout!" (It's true that this winter we are feeding Moondust and several raccoons, in addition to all the birds and squirrels!)

At some point during the evening there are several long telephone calls from whatever members of the family have not been able to make the trip to the Cape this Christmas. It is good to know that the little white farmhouse back in Connecticut is bright with its own holiday festivities, as Connie, Curtis and the girls arrange holly branches on the mantel and light the Yule log. Then we put on some recorded medieval or Renaissance music, or perhaps a few of the old carols, and poke up the fire once more before we go to bed.

When I say good night to the world, I open the door for a moment and look out, sometimes at the dramatic sweep of a snowstorm, sometimes at a clear, quiet sky and dark water, where a single star shines reflected. And I say, as always, "God rest you merry, Gentlemen."

I once said that Christmas is a bridge. We need bridges as the river of time flows past. Today's Christmas should mean creating happy hours for tomorrow and reliving those of yesterday. This year I find myself remembering a Christmas long ago, when Connie was two and her father sat at the piano, holding her on his lap and showing her how to play "Silent Night" with one finger. I remember Jill, who shared Stillmeadow with me for so many years, bright and dark, and her two children, Barbara and David, who tiptoed down one midnight to check for Santa and almost discovered two busy parents instead. Luckily, Star, our first cocker, heard what she thought were burglars on the stairs and raised the alarm.

I think, too, of Hal Borland, who loved this season most of all. Christmas to him meant walking down a snowy road in starlight with Barbara, his wife, and speaking quietly about the birth of Jesus. A carpenter and his wife traveled from Nazareth to Bethlehem. There was no room at the Inn. So the baby was born in the stable and laid to rest in a manger.

Princes and kings and warlords were spreading their power over the lands. What happened to them? Who remembers their deeds? A few historians are knowledgeable about the Roman Empire. But by and large the rulers made no impact. The carpenter's son born in a manger came to speak in simple words to multitudes who listened. He talked about love and justice and the brotherhood of man. And today all over the world, his message sounds as clearly as it did in the hills of Judea. When we light the candles in honor of his birth, our listening hearts fill with hope for peace and love and justice to come.

Sometimes the holiday season is so busy and exciting that the deeper meaning of Christ's birthday is lost. It is good then to walk in the star-filled night, as Hal and Barbara used to do, and touch the real significance of this birthday.

Days pass like melting snowflakes, and before we know it the New Year will be here again. It will be time to make resolutions and to look ahead to the future. But I will still be sorting the memories of the past. Plenty of time to look to the future when spring comes. For now, it is auld lang syne that I think of most.

On New Year's Eve, I set out the big green candle that has burned on the table every December thirty-first for five years now. It comes from Stillmeadow, and its soft glow smells faintly of pine. It is another link with the past.

Evening grows deeper, and the house is peaceful. The new moon dreams in the infinite sky and another year is on the way.

January

January brings a new calendar—in fact, it brings a whole batch of them: scenic calendars, wildlife calendars, pet calendars, recipe calendars, literary calendars, and several that simply say: "Greetings from Your Local Merchant!" It is time now to hang one of the nicest on my kitchen wall and to circle in red the first important dates of the New Year. And as always, I wish once again that April were the first month. For me, the true beginning of the year comes when the first crocus pokes a slender green lancet through the cold earth. But winter has her own values. On a clear January night, the Full Snow Moon silvers the shore. And in the afternoon, Mill Pond has a special quiet, the curve of the beach empty except for a couple of buttoned-up figures walking the happiest dogs in the neighborhood. The water is a dark blue, the sky laced with clouds. The gulls fly in wide circles, and their haunting cries are the true music of the narrow land.

And sometimes now the air is soft and warm and the sun lingers along a sapphire sky. The edge of ice on Mill Pond begins to melt. The days lengthen. We feel it is a promise from spring, a love letter from April: "I'll be coming!"

Meanwhile, January belongs in our climate and we belong to her.

As I throw out the old calendars and establish the new ones, I feel a bit strange. What do they really mean? The biggest one is on the kitchen cabinet, supported by freezer tape. It is easy to jot initials or times in the right squares. Deciphering the messages is a different affair. Does P mean plumber or Philip (the carpenter) or PM? Does 9 mean 9 A.M. or 9 P.M.? You might think that the rest of the note would give a clue but it seldom does: "Call P9," it says. It is a problem too to keep the calendar in place, since the tape gets tired after a while and gives up. You can add a couple of tiny magnets shaped like vegetables, which will help unless they are jarred out of position. In any case, putting up a new calendar gives a fine sense of efficiency.

This year begins with a special excitement in our neighborhood. Helen and Vicky's new housemate, their Irish setter puppy, Hollyberry Red Arrow, is celebrating her first New Year. Holly has a pedigree three pages long, starred with Ch., Double Ch., CDX, UD, and so on, none of which impresses her. She is too busy retrieving anything available. Retrieving, she feels, is her heritage. She can retrieve a letter from the coffee table and skim across the room with it in three seconds flat. When the missive is extracted from her mouth, the envelope is dry (no slobbering) and, although a few bits may trail across the carpet, the return address is undamaged.

Holly has a sturdy but graceful body, beautiful firm well-muscled legs (so rare in setters nowadays), a fine sloping neck, and a strong wide muzzle. The silky ears are set well, just below the crown, and what is called "the bump of elegance" is visible at the back of the head. When she levitates to your lap, you feel the silky down of her mahogany fur (growing darker by the week). Like the Irish I have owned, she smells of a hayfield, just greening. If I were blindfolded I could identify that sweet fragrance.

Finally, when she is scrubbing the powder from my face with a velvety tongue, she looks into my eyes. At this point, words fail me.

The story behind the advent of Holly shows once again the relationship between the past and the present. For when Helen and Vicky began a long friendship with me, it was mainly because of my own Irish setter, Champion Stillmeadow Hollyberry Red. She had won her Obedience Utility Dog and Tracking degrees and had settled down to a life of clamming on the beach, retrieving every dead fish from the town landing, and swimming halfway across Mill Pond. She also visited Helen and Vicky in their rented cottage and had no trouble persuading them that she needed a taste of liverwurst, now and then, and explaining that she enjoyed ice cubes. One day they brought her home to Still Cove and stayed for a drink. We have been friends ever since. When Holly ended her sixteen years, they shared our grief. And they agreed that the minute they moved permanently to the Cape, they would have an Irish "just like Holly." They even went so far as to decide that when they built their own house, they would call it Holly Hill.

Now Stu and Russ Crosby have built a fence enclosing a comfortable yard for the lively tail-flying owner of Holly Hill. She sleeps in the kitchen in her own bed (but when she can manage the stairs leading up to the bedrooms, who knows?).

So a new resident in our neighborhood helps the coming year seem full of brightness as she skips ahead leading us. Already she and Olive's ebullient Cairn, Fergus, have explored every bit of shrubbery and barked at every squirrel. Fergus is two now and rollicking through life as if it were a continual party.

Most of our area is well furnished with dogs and cats. And it is peaceful too. Jean and Andy Russell have a gentle dog, Lucifer, and a charming cat, Seaweed. She and Olive's black cat, Spunky, are great pals. In fact, one day Seaweed came all the way from home to march into Olive's, climb down to the cellar, and use the litter tray. Barbara and Slim's miniature dachshund, Braun, is completely endearing. Millie and Ed have two cats, Sam, a stalwart ebony hunter, and "the other one," a handsome stray who has found warmth enough at Millie and Ed's to take the terror from life. Linda's springer, Miss Boo, is a general favorite and Mrs. Toomey's golden retriever, Honey, is her best friend. My next-door neighbor, Pret, walks his pedigreed Sheltie, Timmie, around Mill Pond rain, shine, wind, snow. I like to watch him striding rapidly along with Timmy bouncing around him.

The Morrisons' Cricket belongs to the Irish group and visits Still Cove daily. Finally, Nancy has a senior citizen, Heidi, a perfect lady, and a small schnauzer named Percy who is a perfect gentleman but has the idea that his mistress is away too much and cries lustily when she comes home.

Olive's seal-point Siamese, whose name is simply Boy, and my Abyssinian, Amber, don't exactly bring up the rear in the registry. Both are conscious of their royal position. Boy is definitely the King of Topside, and Fergus and Spunky realize it. He is an exceptionally loving Siamese and sits on every available lap. He likes to help Olive run the house by accompanying her looped about her neck like a fur piece.

Amber has no competition at our house except the typewriter. When I have worked long enough, she finds that sitting on the carriage diverts my attention. Sitting on my lap is also fine, because then I have to reach one finger over her pointed ears to type and I soon give up. Often she decides to paw the keys herself (a challenge for the scientist who might try to teach her the alphabet).

As I write this, the pale light of dusk is filling the sky. Looking out of the window, I can see an apple-blossom snow spilling on the junipers. Another day of this young January is moving into night. By morning, the snow will have changed the shape of the land. But the past is not buried: part of it is with us, the shining memories as well as the shadowed. A certain royal Irish seems to drift through Still Cove while the lamplight glows on the burnished copper of a very young

puppy who looks exactly like the portrait of Stillmeadow
Holly at four months: big floppy paws, straight long legs,
slender body, wind-blown ears, proud muzzle. And the eyes,
deep with the mystery of life. The birthday gift is a small
silver bowl. The suitable engraving catches a flicker of light:
Holly Two.

So the yesterdays are linked to tomorrow as our puppy
leaps ahead into the future.

Happy New Year!

At noon today the falling snow brought a twilight to the
town. Inside, the house was full of shadows. The windows
on the north side were clouded with white. Those of us who
could change our schedules decided to make a couple of
phone calls, heat up the coffee, and light the fire in the fireplace. Traveler's advisory notices filled the air.

It is midwinter, the season of storms, and we accept the
weather with as much grace as possible—at least, as long as
everything goes smoothly. But when the telephone is out
of order and the electricity blacks out, serenity ebbs away.
We depend on the services we are used to. Without them,
we begin to feel insecure. We do not expect our services
to go off. Conversation gets snappy. Why doesn't the phone
company get the power on? The electric company ought to
be reorganized. The bills go up monthly but the current stays
off hours at a time.

We tend to take so much for granted. When the telephone
rings again, we feel it is high time. Yet repairing the telephone
connections involves crews on call for emergencies, day or
night. The school for training the pole men is in Framingham,
and a week's hard work teaches the prospective crewmen
the skills of climbing tall poles without the extension ladders
and huge machines that tree men use. Pole men wear a safety
belt and, around their calves, buckled straps which fasten
pointed steel gaffs to the shoes. When the men climb a pole,

these gaffs pierce the wood and provide support. There are cases, though, when the pole has been climbed too often and the wood has been gouged out. Then the gaffs do not hold.

The traditional saying in this field is, "Every man has to fall once." It is almost like a slogan. I heard about one such accident from the wife of the man involved.

"He fell twenty-five feet," she said. "He was out of work for a year. It was just before our son was born."

I asked how she felt about his work.

"What can I say? He went right back as soon as he could. They say that is the way to do it. I try not to think what's happening when he is off working. But another man fell forty feet when they were on the same job. And the man at the top was repairing wires—the rubber insulation was off one of them, so he got electrocuted."

It is difficult not to be able to make a long-distance call to Connie when the East is hit by one of the spectacular January storms. But that is the time to think about the snow-deep roads strewn with fallen wires and about the valiant men at work making repairs.

Restoring the electricity, which is really our lifeline, also involves emergency work in blizzards and hurricanes. The year-round hazards of police work are common news. And the fire department protects our town no matter what the weather and seldom battles a conflagration without one or two of the crew having a quick ride to the Cape Cod hospital.

I have a vivid memory of the January night in Connecticut when our barn burned down. The volunteer fire department worked all night. From time to time a few people came in the house to stand on the hearth when their clothes were frozen stiff. The old slab of fieldstone became a small pond. Then back they went outside. The house itself was saved only because they would not give in.

Perhaps the main purpose of the bleak and bitter winter

is to bring a message from nature. Are we really ever independent? Hardly. As the snow falls, our community is protected by those members who *choose* to be out working day and night to keep us comfortable and secure.

Sometimes, of course, the house is filled with friends when the power fails. Candles and oil lamps help out. The fireplace sends a cozy glow (in spite of the fact that so much of the heat goes up the chimney). It is not good to open the refrigerator, and our curious habit of quaffing iced drinks in zero weather must be abandoned, but a Sterno stove heats water for tea. We manage very well.

In January, weekend visitors are few, but some hardy souls brave the hazards and cross the bridge. This involves much telephoning back and forth.

"If that big blizzard hits, we won't try to come."

"Boston reports clearing."

"We may fly to Hyannis and rent a car. Or we may drive from home."

"Just let us know."

"No way of telling when we'll get off. If we drive and run into a bad storm, we'll phone from the Mass Pike."

"All right, we'll look for you whenever you get here."

Now we call WVLC incessantly for up-to-the-minute weather reports, or ask an old-time fisherman what's coming, or gamble by making up the extra beds, convertible sofas, and folding cots. Shall we stock up with a lot of food? Or plan on eating out? (I generally opt for staying at home.)

The suspense is wearing, but nine times out of ten, one way or another, our loved ones do make it. If not, Nancy Colbert turns up to wrestle with closing the sofa beds again. Nancy, who keeps Still Cove on an even keel, is undaunted by any challenge. (The convertibles are supposed to unfold and fold up at the touch of a finger, which they did at the furniture store. But ever since they arrived here, they have absolutely refused to budge without incredible pulling and heaving.) The guest towels are put away again, the limp roses thrown out. Then we open the refrigerator door. Two dozen eggs, six grapefruit, extra quarts of milk, packages of English muffins, four kinds of cheese, bottles of soft drinks (they, at least, will keep, thank goodness). If we are lucky, the neighbors will be able to use some of the perishables—unless they, too, were expecting guests this weekend!

When the guests do arrive, the air bubbles with excitement. If they have never been on Cape in midwinter, they are dazzled by how beautiful it is. The clean sharpness of the wind, the glittering rim of ice around Mill Pond, the closeness of the stars, and, above all, the perfect quiet.

"I never dreamed it would be like this!"

Once the transportation problems for winter guests have been solved, a final question (which actually applies to any time of year but seems more urgent in winter) remains: Why is it always weekends when things go wrong?

My friends and I have never solved this, and I doubt whether any home expert can. For instance, the first time my New York editor flew in to see me, the toilet in the guest bathroom stopped working. The bathroom was all ready for company: freshly laundered curtains, new shower mat, elegant linen hand towels with seahorses embroidered on them, new bars of Old English Lavender—everything, in fact, but a toilet that worked. Fortunately this crisis was solved when Olive dropped in to see if I needed anything.

"Give me a coat hanger," she said. "I want a wire one."

Fifteen minutes later, when my editor walked in, the bathroom was in perfect shape.

Another Saturday, during an August heat spell, four guests drove in from New Jersey, hot, tired, thirsty. At that minute not one drop of water came from a single faucet. The intake valve in the well had become clogged with sand, and in the end Larry Baker had to dig a new well because the pipe could not be pulled. Meanwhile, jugs of water from neighbors were the best we could provide. But why did the well have to give up on a Saturday afternoon? It had been pouring sweet cold water at the touch of a faucet, week in, week out. Why not stop on a Tuesday so the new well could be dug by the weekend? Why?

It was an autumn Sunday when Barbara and her husband, Val, came from New York. They had to leave the next day, but we planned a long leisurely drive over the winding country roads with gold, soft red, russet glowing across the landscape. Instead, Val spent half the day running up and down the cellar stairs working on the water tank, which was airbound. "Never mind," he said cheerfully. "Actually, I enjoy household chores like this." But was it air-bound Thursday or Friday? No, it waited until Sunday.

Now here is a curious fact. Thursday is not the weekend, but when it is Thanksgiving, it has the same effect on the mechanics of living. For it was Thanksgiving Day when the furnace went off and a houseful of guests shivered by the fire until Willie Gallant left his own dinner in Brewster and rushed to the rescue. Remember this was only Thursday, but it was a holiday.

Perhaps the most dramatic episode was when Olive, who was then still living in New Jersey for most of the year, came for a weekend visit with her Siamese cat and Trinka, the miniature schnauzer (who died last year). My Abyssinian was not noted for sociability, especially to strange animals, so when we decided to go to The Cleaver for some charcoal-broiled steak, we shut Amber in my bedroom, put the Siamese in the den, and left Trinka on her security blanket in the living room. (I have told this story before but as Olive says, it is worth retelling.)

It was a black, cold night with the rain already sluicing down, but the house was warm and we left all the lights on. Our threesome would surely be snug and tranquil until we got back.

We had a lovely dinner, saving enough steak for those at home. Driving down Tonset, we noticed that the neighborhood seemed darker than usual, but we decided that everyone had gone out to dinner just as we had on this bleak night.

When we reached Still Cove, however, we saw that the yard light was out. We sloshed to the front door and opened it with a bang. The house was black as a pit and still as a cave. When a pocket flashlight went on, we saw with dismay that every door inside was wide open. The ominous stillness paralyzed us.

"They've killed themselves!" I gasped.

By the time candles flickered into life, we found them. Trinka yawned from the hearth; Amber was tucked in my bed; the Siamese came out of the den twitching his tail and inquiring about snacks. An hour later when the current came on again, we calmed ourselves with hot toddies. Left alone in the storm, our temperamental darlings had been peaceful as doves!

Such crises become amusing afterward, and we often go over them. But the unanswered question still haunts me: Why is it always weekends?

In this neighborhood, winter entertaining is casual. Get-togethers are simple and flexible. Barbara calls up to say that Slim will pick me up for supper. But if we have a blizzard, we can always make it the next night—the casserole will keep. If I am snowed in, Jan and Gail may decide to bring the dinner over, since they have a four-wheel drive and weather is no problem. While they unpack the meal, Jan has only to heat the rolls. Gail builds up the fire and puts up the tray tables. The menu itself is just as simple. But nothing in summertime compares with creamy oyster stew, crisp salad, and hot buttered rolls, while the sea wind rattles the windows and the hearth fire adds a warm glow to the room.

Then on bright clear days we can walk in the pine woods. If there is a layer of snow, we follow the tracks of the winter people: squirrel trails, the long skunk patterns, sometimes the sharp imprint of a deer's hoof, and always some we cannot identify. The whole story of winter wildlife is visible. On the way back, we gather evergreen branches to fill the old bean pot on the hearth.

"Oh, Gram, I wish we could stay all winter," says my granddaughter Anne.

"How soon can we come back?" asks Alice.

Waking to a blizzard, I thought it was still night but Amber assured me it was time to have breakfast. Indeed, it was ten fifteen. As I poured the orange juice, I tried to observe the difference between the light on such a day and that in a summer storm. Today the house inside is dark, a kind of grey twilight laced with deeper shadows. But the world outside—sea, sky, evergreen shores—is veiled with snow spilling down. It has a different look, a white darkness. So inside, the lights must be on, but when I open the door to check on the birds, I blink my eyes.

At breakfast Amber and I watched the few brave cardinals and three blue jays and our one mockingbird clawing away to scrape seeds from under the snow. They faced into the gale wind just as the five boats left in Mill Pond did. I told Amber that if I would only face my troubles as the birds and boats do, I would survive the storms much better than by turning my back.

I spent the morning on the mail, including a letter to an Orleans boy who after graduating from high school applied to the Navy because "I want to get more education, and this way I can earn something while I'm doing it." The only problem was a day in Hyannis sitting around at the recruiting office with no food. He drank fifteen Cokes and never one again at my house. Now he is on his first tour of duty, on an island somewhere in the Indian Ocean.

I first knew Glenn when he came on his bicycle to ask if we could use someone to do chores after school. He was a thin, leggy, dark-haired boy with very bright eyes and a mouth ready to smile. Inside of one day, he had become part of the household. He never said, "What shall I do now?" He looked around, noticed what needed to be done, and set to work. He shoveled paths in the snowy yard, cleaned the fireplace whenever he thought the ashes were too deep, filled the woodbox, cleaned the garage, and, for fun, washed and polished the car. In bad winter days, he walked from his house on Brick Hill Road. But he always came.

So now I try to figure out the twelve initials on his last address plus the three numbers. I know that NMCB means Naval Mobile Construction Battalion. The rest is a mystery. My letter will go to an island fifteen thousand miles from the United States. Glenn reports that the ocean around it is light blue, beautiful but full of sharks and barracuda, so risky for swimming. The island is beautiful too, with palm trees, coconuts, and many birds. The only animals are a few wild horses and hundreds of donkeys and chickens, plus a few cats. The temperature is 110 degrees.

The work schedule is eleven hours a day, five days a week, and six hours on Saturday. Obviously the United States Navy is not sitting quietly in home bases. The island is in the Indian Ocean, which is the nearest base to Iran.

This gives me a great deal to think about. I do not know how many boys like Glenn enlisted in the Navy that same year. But I do know that they came from homes all over the country—the flat midwestern cornfields, the rolling blue hills of the South, the golden West. This one left Cape Cod, the place where he could swim in the cold water, fish from a small boat, go clamming.

Does he belong on that steaming tropical island so far from

home? Do the other young men belong there? Their generation is terribly divided, it seems to me. A dangerously large segment is involved with drugs, alcoholism, crime (including arson, rape, murder). Vandalism is so common it is now accepted. This segment of the future society is destructive, and unless we manage to change it, the next decades will demolish us.

Yet Glenn and his friends represent the traditional American: energetic, ambitious, focused, responsible. We need them. If we are swept into another war to end wars, we will destroy the very ones who would build a solid foundation for a better world. I have lived through two major wars. During the first one, I was far too young to question anyone, but when the president of our high school class had his head blown off in the Argonne, I felt it was a bitter waste for him to become only one more body to bury. He could have contributed so much. Now I think it is a waste for any life to be needlessly sacrificed.

In the second war, I was mature enough to be an air raid warden in New York City. With the great brilliant metropolis smothered in blackness, we walked the streets watching the night sky for the bombers that might sweep in and make our city a rubble heap. The extent of my services was to trust a very dubious elevator to the sixth floor of a shabby apartment building and tell Mrs. Weissmuller that her blackout window drape had a slit in it. Since her oldest son was on the battlefront, I did not feel she was signaling to those bombers!

Now in this January of a new decade, I wonder whether the world is really on the edge of another war. What would happen if all the populations on the planet simply refused to fight human beings they did not even know?

I know I cannot be a pacifist, but neither can I believe war is the great solution, since the wars I have known did not bring permanent peace, in spite of all the horror, annihilation, death. Here we are again at the point of pouring billions of dollars and a generation of men into another conflict. We walk in fear, but some of us remember a time when war was something to read about in history books.

I would not wish Glenn and his fellow members in the United States armed forces to change their minds about serving their country. Glenn says, "Whatever we do, it is for serving the country." Yet I wish they were able to come home.

As I seal my letter to him, I go to the door. The storm now displays the full magnificence of nature. It is our part to accept it. For winter's lease will soon run out and the soft breeze will smell of lilacs.

The white blindness of snow is a warning that winter is definitely in full sway, but the pattern changes at one special time. The January thaw suddenly arrives. It is like an island in the sea of winter. We never know whether it will last a day or a week or ten days. But while it is here, the wind gentles, dark clouds move out to sea, the air is soft and smells sweet as the snowmelt begins. The sun, the blessed sun, shines over our small piece of the planet.

My friend Hal Borland used to say it was as if spring opened a door briefly. Gardeners rush out to poke into the soil to see how far down it is frozen solid and then go back indoors to study seed catalogs. Homemakers insist on taking off a few storm windows so fresh air sweeps the mustiness from the house. The smell of drying mittens, damp jackets, and soggy boots gives way to the scent of salt and pine.

Out we go to the beaches to watch the calming sea and to drive past the marshes, now cinnamon-colored in the pale sunlight. We spend time at Fort Hill looking down on streams winding their way through tawny grasses to the sea beyond. This is the place where eternity seems tangible.

While the thaw lasts, the town is bright with colors as

people catch up with all the errands that were postponed because of bad weather. Friends stop on the corner to visit instead of scuttling before the wind. Watson's is already turning toward the coming season with the latest spring fashions. Meanwhile, thrifty shoppers stock their wardrobes with winter coats, storm jackets, and warm slacks now reduced.

The days grow longer now, and how comfortable this is! I do not know anyone who enjoys having night set in at four twenty. For me, it chops up the working day. My typewriter is at the end of the study, with a wall of windows beside it. They face the west, overlooking the potato patch, a mass of wild rosebushes, the thickest piney woods, and a wide sweep of sky saved for sunset. The windows in the front wall look to the bluff, with Mill Pond rippling below. In summer, sunshine fills the room until late afternoon, and then the brilliant coral and gold of sunset flows in from the west. On the middle ledge of the windows are seven spun-glass unicorns and two cranberry-glass wine goblets. The light sparkling through the crystal inspires me to keep working until six, six thirty, seven—why not?

But now, in winter, shadows begin to fall on the harvest table that serves as my desk about teatime. The waters of Mill Pond absorb the light. Dusk sifts on the spun-glass figures and the ruby wineglasses. It cannot be time to start supper. At that moment, a last bar of sun falls on a small four-footed person walking in from the living room. She comes to the table, sits down, and fixes a steady gaze on me.

"Amber, it's too early to eat."

A negative switch of a seal-dark tail answers.

Three times she circles the typewriter, purring persuasively. Then to my lap and over to the top of the typewriter and she sits.

"I'll be done in a few minutes."

One velvet paw reaches down to tap a key.

It's time to turn the lights on anyway. "But Amber, we can't have supper at five fifteen. I'll give you a snack."

By the time we reach the kitchen, I too am hungry. When I open the refrigerator door, approval purrs all over the room. We will be eating long before the cardinals and jays and mockingbirds and squirrels have called it a day. And I reflect that because night begins too early, I am actually short two hours: I have lost the stretch from four to six. Perhaps most people are not as affected by daylight and their schedules do not change. But as winter moves along, Amber and I begin to count how many minutes are added to daylight.

Early morning brings a blaze of gold in the sky above Nauset. When it is very cold, colors seem intensified. Mill Pond is a deeper blue. The foam edging along the shore is whiter than yesterday's snow. The yard is vivid as five cardinals swoop in from the junipers. They are brighter this year than ever. I have asked everybody I know and everyone agrees, which is odd in itself for there is usually one in any group who must disagree. But this January, the sleek scarlet bodies flame with color. Even the lady cardinals glow against the soft tan of the dried grass.

The blue jays bullet in from the cedars, and their forget-me-not blue and white adds to the display. Then a scattering of strangers crowd in. I can't identify them. They are small birds, grey or brown. I am only close enough to see their tails tip up and down. The only trouble with Peterson's guide is that it is difficult to find a bird when you cannot get a good look at it. (I do have field glasses but never seem able to focus them in time, so I've given them up.)

Tiny Tim, my resident squirrel, joins the early breakfast. He has been a lesson to me. I never had a chance to watch a squirrel before, not even in Connecticut, where we had thirty grey squirrels driving us quite mad. But here there is food enough for all, and Tiny Tim and the bird bevy get along amiably, as do the twenty-two quail. Then, too, the feeder is an easy distance from the kitchen window. Squirrel-watching is easy.

Tiny Tim is not much bigger than Jimmy DeLory's "chippies," who can sit comfortably in his hand. Tim's red coat has darkened with winter so that now it is deep russet. He has gained some weight since he first moved in. But his flying grace is the same. He is so airborne that I expect him to soar like a miniature kite in the first good breeze. To get from the split-rail fence to the ground he spins into the air, tail whirling. He would not dream of just stepping to the fencepost and climbing down. Air skimming is quicker.

When he has eaten enough cracked corn, birdseed, bread cubes, nuts, he tips his little pointed face up, whisks his tail two or three times, and leaps to the fence post in a lovely arc of flight, to the half grapefruit nailed there. He flattens himself, stomach down, and serves himself dessert by digging into the juicy pulp. When the birdbath is not frozen, he leaps down to the ground beside it, stands on tiptoes to reach the rim, and drinks lustily. Mealtime over, Tim disappears into the evergreen labyrinth somewhere near the wild pear tree.

Like all year-round Cape Codders, I am used to the typical question from vacationers.

"What do you do in winter?"

"I study a red squirrel," I answer.

Nature does not pack up and take off across the bridge when summer ends. Instead, the bounty of autumn, the adventure of winter, the magic of early spring are all here as usual. This is why I think Cape Codders are basically happy people. Even those whose ancestors did not land in Provincetown but who have lived here most of their lives seem to have an optimistic outlook and a philosophy that makes nervous breakdowns rare. If the world is coming to an end, we'll do what we can. But I heard the loons the other night— may mean an early spring.

February

"Well, it's a short month," Olive says, with her usual optimism.

"Not short enough," I remark.

To me, February is like standing in the middle of a bridge. December and January are behind, but it is a long journey to the other side where daffodils scatter gold on the greening shore. On the other hand, I would never want to go away to the summer ease of Florida or the mellow skies of California. Instead, I check the woodpile to be sure I don't need to call Stu and Russ Crosby. I once read an article in my favorite *Country Journal* about the correct method of measuring cords of wood; I rely on guesswork and decide another half cord should about do it.

I remind Amber that March is ahead, and in my opinion, March is the worst month in New England, even worse than February. It seems as if nature is unwilling to let go of winter. Meanwhile, it is time to restock staples when the wild sea wind ebbs, ask Jimmy DeLory to check the car, get another twenty-five pounds of birdseed, and do all the household chores left undone since Christmas.

This past week, one difficult chore was finished, that of organizing the bookshelves. Even with the help of Nancy and Olive, it was a struggle, almost enough to make me despair. When all the books are on the floor for sorting, I am convinced that they will never fit back into the floor-to-ceiling shelves in my workroom and living room. There are neat stacks of poetry books, country books, animal books, mysteries, research volumes. One whole shelf is filled with Hal Borland's priceless work. But the sofa is drowned in books which do not fall into any special category, such as the delightful Miss Read volumes and Katherine Mansfield's *Letters*.

I think my fellow organizers would prefer to have me go away, because all I do is dip into any book they give me and start to reread it. My final conclusion is that I should not have written so many books myself, so I suggest that we stop—wade out between the stacks, clear off some chairs, and have a cup of tea. Just forget the whole business.

On the other hand, we do not notice the black snow clouds gathering outside because we are in the magic world of literature, which has nothing to do with weather at all. (Unless, of course, you read about climbing the Himalayas or crossing the Sahara in a sandstorm.)

One special book I laid aside to reread later was *The Wonders of the Invisible World* by my ancestor, Cotton Mather, with the added *A Farther Account of the Tryals of the New England Witches* by his father, Increase Mather, D.D. Originally written in 1693, it was published in England in 1862. I am glad to say historians have now discovered that the Reverend Cotton in the end had a big part in stopping witch trials. The engraving in the frontispiece shows a bewigged, rather pleasant man. I asked Olive if I looked like him.

"I hope not," Olive commented.

One sad thing about this era is that the habit of reading has diminished. Everyone agrees that the world of books is fascinating, enlarges our horizons, gives a kind of enjoyment nothing else can provide, but somehow people seldom get around to actually opening a book.

I am not one to blame parents or teachers for the fact that so many children do not read, but too often we hear,

"I don't have anything to do." Listening to disco records may kill time (while deafening the ears), but it doesn't really enrich life. And while some television programs are, in their way, masterpieces, many are pure junk. It's meager fare for young minds. Yet often, the parents themselves say, "I never have time to read."

It seems to me that the habit should begin when children are small. I think even those teenagers who drift around in gangs and enliven the dullness of existence by tossing cherry bombs, looting, or getting "high" in one way or another could find excitement spending a few hours sharing the magic of books. Incidentally, their conversation would not be limited to "Yeah, uh huh, yup."

In any case, the job of sorting my own books was finally done. It will be months before I learn to find things again— I never had any problem with the old helter-skelter arrangement because I knew by instinct that the Keats biography would probably be next to the book on flowers in Shakespeare—but the new system will make it possible for other people, friends and relatives with normally logical minds, to locate a book without a two-hour search. And the shelves have been cleared of what one critic called the literary flotsam and jetsam, so there is room, at last, to add some new treasures.

Olive poked up the fire, while Nancy went to the kitchen to bring out cheese and crackers. The winter sunset was touching Mill Pond with gold, and peace settled back.

It is comforting to reflect that nature herself keeps her accustomed rhythms. We have the security of knowing that no matter what happens in our human lives, the early migratory birds will be dropping down at Still Cove some cold pale morning just as they always have. And the first nubbins of daffodil shoots still poke up by the front door. I am sure no single soul here on Cape Cod really wishes that someone would invent a way to turn February into a tropical paradise.

The winter blue of the sea, the hoot of the snowy owl, and the lengthening twilights are special gifts we treasure.

February is really a short month after all!

The month of the Full Wolf Moon has a special meaning to Cape Codders since February 6, 1978, made history with a storm that overwhelmed this fragile arm of land reaching out to sea. Those of us in residence were, we thought, very well prepared for another winter blizzard. When the wind began howling, I filled jugs of water, found the oil lamps, put candles around, turned up the furnace, opened a can of soup, laid a fire in the fireplace. But nothing could really have prepared us for the actual storm.

Still Cove has some disadvantages during bad weather. The house is at the bottom of a sloping private road. When it snows, the drifts always require Jimmy DeLory's plow, and when heavy rain falls, a flood of water rushes down to turn the driveway into a pond. When the "electric" goes off (which it does any old time, winter or summer), the well pump promptly takes a rest. The beautiful Thermopane picture windows are guaranteed to withstand ninety-five-mile winds, and I am told that it is good for them to shake from fifty-five on. But Amber and I watch them constantly.

"Pull down the blinds," my cousin Rob advised me, "just in case. Then the breaking glass won't crash in on you and Amber."

I told Amber not to worry since we had been through a good many blizzards and a few authentic hurricanes, but about midday she began to wander restlessly around, flicking her tail nervously. The fury of the storm increased, and at three thirty a ninety-three-mile gale was registering. This was more than either of us had bargained for.

Meanwhile, beach dwellers were being evacuated, emergency crews were at work, radio warnings poured in. It was no comfort to hear that the worst blizzard in history had paralyzed Boston and the mainland. Now it was our turn. When the eye of the storm passed over us, there was a taste of honey in the air, but shortly the wind rose again to full blast.

Luckily, Amber and I were safe: our own house stood firm. But everywhere else, homes were swept out to the raging Atlantic, roads vanished, telephone poles crashed. The beaches we knew so well were being destroyed; an unfamiliar seacoast was evolving. Nature was drawing a new map of Cape Cod.

One very special small cottage in North Eastham was tossed into Nauset Marsh. But by then the beautiful marsh was part of the sea. It was a sturdy little building that had withstood many wild winters: the house where Henry Beston spent a year alone studying the mysteries of nature and sharing his discoveries in his matchless book, *The Outermost House.* Just as Thoreau had his Walden Pond, Beston had the sea, the golden dunes, the migratory birds, the gossamer butterflies, and the saltwater creatures. There was more talk about the loss of that little house than of any other disaster brought by the great storm. My neighbor Ed Connors came over a few days later to report that he saw the window frame of the Outermost House floating in the sea when he was walking the beach somewhere near Robert's Cove. He recognized it because he knew the construction. Perhaps if enough pieces turned up, the one-room cottage could be rebuilt.

The Outermost House was published in 1926 and has become a classic. But Henry Beston himself is still something of a mystery. We know that he was not a recluse or even basically a loner. In his book *Herbs and the Earth,* published in 1935, he says that without the help of his wife, Elizabeth Coatsworth Beston, both the manuscript and he himself would still be out in the herb garden. The dedication is to "Two Young Persons who will never pull up or step on Father's herbs." So I picture him as an ardent explorer who chose this particular small area of the planet as his field. The result was a gift to the future.

After the colossal storm, the Cape, with customary courage, began the task of restoring as much as possible. The contours of the beaches will never be the same, bits of houses will float in the sea for a long time, old waterways are gone from the marshes. But the first thing visitors ask will always be "Where was it that the Outermost House used to stand?"

Which means to me that there are some things no storm can erase.

The latest nor'easter will not go down in history, as did the catastrophe of 1978, but I called it a "complete storm." Rain hammered against the windows from midnight on. The only way to be sure it was not sleet was to turn on the yard light. When I opened the door a crack, was it water or ice falling in my hand? The wind sounded like a full orchestra with cymbals as well as bass viols.

By morning the sound of the surf at Nauset added a new rhythm. Mill Pond echoed the great waves in its lesser realm. The air was opaque, the sky flat. When I looked out, Grand View across the pond was erased from sight. On the near side, cedars and junipers swayed, but no branches fell. I told Amber that if we had the flexibility of those trees, we would be better off.

At least the birds would have fresh water in every puddle. My mockingbird is an insatiable drinker and bather. During dry spells he sits on the split-rail fence and stares at the kitchen window. If there is no reaction, his voice mounts and mounts. Often Nancy puts down her glass of iced tea (winter or summer) and rushes out with a pan of water.

"He says he can't stand it," she reports.

This recent storm sent me to the telephone to tell Janie that I couldn't get to the beauty shop. Then I spoke to Olive, whose snug house is around the corner from Still Cove.

"Well, I do have a few leaks," she said calmly. "And it's raining down the chimney again. The cellar has water coming in that same corner. The sliding doors are leaking. So I'll be busy. See you later."

"Have you heard from Helen and Vicky yet?"

"They just called. Holly Two won't go out of the house. Won't even put a paw out."

This surprised me because I remembered how Holly One, my own Irish setter, had loved storms. Most of all she loved a good blizzard. She would race through the falling snow, then lie down in a snowbank and bask when the sun came out. But I realized suddenly that Holly Two is not quite four months old. She is a big rangy girl but weighs only twenty-six pounds. My Holly tipped the scales at sixty-five when she was grown. One of our Cape gales could whip up that puppy as easily as it does the sprig of oak with four dry leaves that is skittering across the yard.

When my Holly came in from greeting the storm, she wore pearls of snow tangled in the plumes of her tail and ice nuggets between her toes. I would rush for a warm towel, but she would fling herself down by the fire with a sigh of satisfaction and melt puddles on the hearthstone.

For an Irish, nothing brightens a dark winter day like a few good bounces in a snowdrift. Second best is a slippery walk in the mud. Here in New England, we wait for that time in February when the air warms for a day or two, the fringe of icicles along the eaves begins to drip steadily, and the frozen ground thaws here and there to mud. This is the time when a treasure-hunting dog can find all sorts of lovely things that have been buried under the snow: my granddaughter Anne's red mitten, matted with burrs; somebody's key ring with a single key (A key ring? lost in our front yard? Whose could it be? The mystery will keep us guessing for weeks but never be solved); a flattened dog-food can that must have slipped out of the garbage pail when the raccoons tipped it over and unlatched the lid; a half-chewed tennis ball, still frozen solid. Holly's impulse was always to share whatever lovely surprise she excavated from the muddy slush, and we tried to appreciate her generosity as we sneaked the rusty sardine tin back into the garbage pail or pulled from the pillow an aged beef bone. Besides, I've always maintained that if I had to choose between a spotless house and a happy dog, I would not hesitate to choose the latter. And come to think of it, I did make this choice years ago when our first cocker spaniel, a round ebony puppy named Star, lugged into the freshly scrubbed kitchen a smelly old boot twice her size that she had found in the swamp. I have never for one moment regretted it either.

For a sensible cat like Amber, of course, both stormy weather and brief periods of thaw are good times to stay indoors, paws dry, fur hot from a long nap on the hearth. I feel the same way. There was a time when I loved to ice-skate on our Connecticut pond, pushing an aluminum lawn chair ahead of me for balance, or go crunching along the snowy path up the hill to the old orchard. But nowadays, I enjoy my winter weather through the picture window.

The grandchildren wind themselves up in wool scarves and dash out for a walk on the windy beach. I stay indoors with a fire, some red apples, and a mug of something warm to drink. The traditional potion for a cold evening is hot buttered rum. I've read somewhere that the Pilgrims made it in a huge pewter bowl and heated it by plunging in a hot iron called a loggerhead. My own favorite recipe is not so dramatic. It calls for individual mugs, heated first. Into each one you put 1 teaspoon confectioner's sugar, ¼ cup rum, and 1 tablespoon butter. Then add ½ cup boiling water, top with a sprinkle of nutmeg or cinnamon, and take a sip that will warm you right down to your toes.

Cider heated with a piece of stick cinnamon makes an encouraging winter drink too, and so does extra-rich hot chocolate made with a dash of coffee and a whisk of vanilla or a lacing of warm brandy or Irish whiskey. The brandy or whiskey blends well with black coffee, too, topped with a fluff of whipped cream. Then let the February wind whistle all it likes down the chimney!

The first sign of spring is the skunk cabbage, thrusting emerald spears through icy ground. Once, a long time ago, I asked Hal Borland to explain this phenomenon. It seems that plants generate their own heat and exude it. Skunk cabbage may generate as much as 27 degrees of heat and so is able to keep right on growing even in a frosting of snow. But why does skunk cabbage decide to make the effort around the end of February? I find this still a mystery.

Groundhog Day is another. Who first decided that woodchucks really knew how much longer winter would last? Most legends have some basis in fact, but I believe woodchucks may just get tired of the old burrow and feel hungry and pop up for a look. It must feel good to rouse from hibernation and taste fresh air again.

Valentine's Day is still a pleasant holiday, although not as romantic as it once was. Whoever decided that comic valentines were a good idea should have been sent away to think it over. Nothing can ever match the old-fashioned cards, the lovely billets-doux with plump rosy hearts, bluebirds perching dizzily on garlands of violets, and the inevitable verses inside sighing of love. The signature was always *Guess Who?* and the excitement of identifying the handwriting added to the enjoyment.

"I know you sent it!"

"What makes you think so?"

"It's your handwriting. It's the same as on that note asking for a date to the skating party."

"You mean you saved that note?"

"That was the first time you put your arms around me. My right skate fell off."

This year's Valentine mail brought a huge flowery card signed *Betty, San Francisco, 1967*. With it came a note of explanation (but no indication of who Betty was or of whether or not she and I had ever met).

I was cleaning out the desk today, the note said, *and I found this. It's on its way at last. Happy 1980!*

So many modern Valentines attempt to be funny. "Hi yah, kid, don't kid me," "I have a thing for you," or something equally inspiring. More romantic donors do send red heart-shaped boxes filled with sweet chocolates and cards saying briefly, "Sweets to the Sweet." But the mixture of romance and mystery is gone.

All the same, some things remain. Customs may change, but if you go to Rock Harbor to watch the cold beauty of winter sunset, you are still likely to see a long-legged boy and slim girl racing along the shining sand, hand in hand. They are not looking at the sunset; they look at each other. When they stop for breath, he tosses her wind-blown hair aside, and the two silhouettes merge into one just as the sea turns gold. Romance does not change, fashion or no fashion.

Happy Valentine's Day still belongs to the young in heart!

On a wintry afternoon my trip begins by driving up Mill Pond Road past Orin Tovrov's stately white mansion and on to Tonset Road. Long ago this driveway was where carriages drove vacationers on golden summer days. I am told they came by train from Boston to Orleans. The remains of the roadbed are now a subject of controversy. Does the Cape need train service? Should a bicycle trail be built? How about another highway?

I like to think of elegant ladies and gentlemen climbing

from the carriages, dining, strolling on the cool green lawns, or possibly playing croquet in the leafy shade. The women wore long flowing dresses; the men were decorously clad. Afternoon tea may have been served as shadows lengthened. It sounds so tranquil!

Along Tonset are some old houses, some new; there are still stretches of piney woods, now silvered with snow. The cemetery hill rises gently, the gravestones punctuating the snow. The whole history of this ancient town is written here.

Turning right to Main Street, there are more charming old houses, the pleasant new library, the new post office, Compass Rose Book Shop where Dick and Betty Philbrick can find almost any book. We stop at Jimmy DeLory's service station to make a date with Jimmy and Eileen. The corner marks the crossing of Route 6A and Main Street, and even in midwinter traffic is heavy. Route 6A goes on to Province-town, Main Street toward Rock Harbor. Eventually we reach Miss Rogers's Flower Shop. Miss Rogers belongs to memory, but Bill Wildman opens the door and this is our destination. The air is heady with scents and is summer warm. In the greenhouse, color glows down the long beds. The snow has stopped, so pale sunlight falls on purple gloxinias, rosy cyclamens, white African violets (I hope). It is like entering a tropical land, and even if one buys no plants or flowers, the spirit is refreshed.

There is none of the impersonality of a big city florist's. Bill and the staff welcome callers like hosts as they help find just the right plant or flower or make up a bouquet with skillful hands. I look for my favorite delicate coral roses, which Bill assures me are salmon. If I tell him how lucky he is to live in summer all year, he reminds me he is up at dawn to drive to Boston no matter how cold it is. Actually Miss Rogers's follows the seasons, for soon baskets of early bulbs will appear, the poinsettias will be gone, and pots of daffodils and narcissi will fill the shelves.

By the time we leave this island of warmth it is even colder outside. The worst of winter to me is early dark, but when we drive back on Tonset the houses are lighted. Supper lights suggest workers coming home, children dropping wet boots on clean floors, dogs washing snow balls from their toes, cats toasting by the fire, homemakers stirring the savory stew. The lighted houses look happy.

As we turn the corner toward Mill Pond, I see the best sight of all—the lights of Still Cove shining through the darkness.

There are some rare individuals who never lose anything. I find them awesome. No matter how carefully I tuck items away, they vanish. The canceled check I am looking for is no longer in the desk drawer, and it is the only one missing. I count the laundry. One sock is gone. The one book I need is not on the shelf.

Even some of my best-organized friends have the same trouble, especially with keys. It is common here in the Tonset area for the phone to ring at some ungodly hour.

"Have you got a key to my front door? I'm locked out."

Twenty minutes later, I have located enough keys to open five other houses, but not that one. I do find half a dozen unidentifiable keys, plus the long-lost key to the cellar door and the key to a closet we never lock anyway.

If a car key gets locked inside the car, the problem is different. At least the driver knows where the key is; not that this helps much. Now the question is where to find a locksmith or somebody with a crowbar. Of course, this kind of loss seldom happens unless a date with the dentist or doctor is imminent.

It is a mistake, I have discovered, to secrete precious objects. I once put my favorite piece of jewelry in a safe place and then forgot where it was. I hunted for weeks before giving up. Two years later the jewelry turned up in the drawer right where it belonged. I have no idea where it had been in the meanwhile. Also, one of my miniature glass unicorns evidently took off for a stroll in the violets. He is still missing.

The children would say that things disappear because they have been taken temporarily by the Borrowers, those minuscule people described in Mary Norton's books. Some tiny baby has just been born in the household under the floorboards and needs a crib. Your teaspoon is exactly the right size. Sometimes this does seem to be the only possible explanation.

When some friends were discussing their own problems—from the wallet that appeared on the bank counter, after all those charge plates and licenses had been replaced, to the lobster shears that turned up in the refrigerator—we agreed that no matter how much we tried, we would never be able to keep everything in its place. We decided that the solution was to set aside one day a week as Hunting Day and the rest of the time to just get along. This would pile all the stresses into that single day. The rest of the week could be used for a less harried experience. Lost car keys would be the one exception.

Making lists of special items is a help except that it takes extra time to find the list. It may turn up in the back pages of the telephone book. But simply making lists gives you a small feeling of accomplishment—of being a well-organized person. Nobody wants to be called a dreamer.

"Don't keep your head in the clouds," Father used to say whenever he found me lounging at the window.

Even when you are not embarked on a major search for some mislaid treasure, homemaking is never dull. The same cannot be said for every job, it seems to me. When I worked in a magazine office, a lot of time was spent in total confusion because pages 35, 50, and 87 were missing from a manuscript, or the title page of an article due at the printers had been somehow lost. Editing recipes was a steady grind. Was it ¼ teaspoon curry powder or ½? Was it a 350-degree oven or 375? Better settle for "Season to taste" and "Bake in moderate oven." (The author could not be reached: she was somewhere on an island studying native dishes.) The work was sometimes exciting and challenging, but all too often it was merely routine.

But when housework suddenly seems unbearable—as it sometimes does, especially in February—the homemaker has a freedom of choice seldom possible in an office routine. One can choose an hour in the fantasy land of seed catalogs and plan for spring. Let the washing go—it will keep. Or go out to cut juniper branches for the ironstone jug. Take an extra pan of bird food out and watch the quail come bobbing along. Or if your conscience will not let you put off the chores entirely, at least pick a job you really enjoy. Instead of running the vacuum, polish the copper (this always gives a sense of accomplishment).

The main thing about housework is that you can change the routine and make your own choices. One certainty is that if you run a household, you will never be out of projects.

A new recipe is always cheering on a cold night, and one of my recent favorites is Jean Lovdal's Country Baked Spareribs. It calls for 4 to 8 pounds spareribs cracked through the center and cut in pieces, 2 bouillon cubes dissolved in 2 cups boiling water, ¼ cup hot catsup, 3 tablespoons Worcestershire sauce, 1 tablespoon vinegar, ⅛ teaspoon Cayenne pepper, ½ teaspoon celery salt, 3 whole cloves, 3 whole allspice, ½ bay leaf, and 1 medium onion, sliced.

Broil ribs on both sides until browned, drain off fat. Mix all other ingredients together and pour over spareribs. Cover with foil and bake until fork tender—about 2 hours. Serves 4 to 6. It means happy cooking.

After a long bleak period, suddenly the air clears and at night the meadows of the sky blossom with stars . . . A golden leaf of moon drifts over the Mill Pond. The surprise to me is that it is as magical as ever. I have been through many nights of evening stars and young moons after long soggy days, but here is a new adventure! When the phone rings and Barbara's deep singing voice says, "Oh, have you looked out over Mill Pond tonight?" I say, "I was just going to call you. I can't believe it. Ask Slim whether he would like to come over and pick a basket of stars for his greenhouse."

They pop over, and the three of us sit quietly feeling the wonder of nature. What is so special is that we do not comment that the weather is, at last, clearing up and it is a few degrees warmer, or that pretty soon it will be time to put in those early peas, or even that two robins came to Sea View Road yesterday. The latest robberies, fires, and lost dogs are forgotten. Amber is a still silhouette on the dark windowsill. What has happened? The mystery of nature has taken our spirits' sovereignty for a brief period. We shall always remember this eventide.

We forget the news reports, the gossip, the whole debris of life that washed up on our shores, but in difficult hours we shall see again the pale lavender sky diamonded with new stars and with a slender moon gliding over Robert's Cove. Memory will even bring back the silvery ripples on the water.

It is a good idea to collect bright memories. Often when neighbors gather, I notice that the talk focuses on the latest catastrophes. But when the Canada geese fly over or the first redwings arrive, then the conversation sparkles.

"What a lovely afternoon! Aren't we lucky to live on the Cape! I told my husband last night . . ."

Most of us know people who spend their time gathering news to share with friends. Suppose only good news filled their briefcases. It would be a new world.

Here on the Cape, we get the latest news from Boston hot off the breakfast griddle. It doesn't sound like the city

I knew when I was spending years of my life where the breezes from Waban blow gently (that is, they did in spring, but in winter there was nothing gentle about Wellesley). Boston, in those legendary times, was like Athens in the golden days of Greece. When we had permission to go into the city on a Saturday afternoon, the dormitories were a whirlpool of activity. The train always had a bevy of late-comers racing down the platform. In that period, trains would slow down.

My eternal problem was *gloves*. I did not then and do not now wear covering on my hands. But I had a good pair of gloves to wear to Boston. One was always missing. Odd, too, since both lived quietly in my glove box. I carried the left-hand glove.

The charm of Boston made our heads spin. My roommate, Jill, came from Freeport, Illinois, a small farming and lumbering center. I came from a small Wisconsin town noteworthy only because of Houdini, Edna Ferber, and a small liberal arts college which had a true giant grizzly bear in the stuffed-animal room in the museum. Boston, therefore, was an earthly paradise to us. The history alone gave me dizzy spells: real history, but our own, not the history of the great wall of China. I felt I should walk softly. Winter and summer, streets were real and did not vanish when we went up and down, down and up. Coming from Paul Revere's world, we absorbed the Louisa Alcott time. We bought pickled limes from a street barrel just as Amy did. I still remember the excitement as well as the sharp clean tang.

The ease with which I decided to save the last pickled lime and go on to the Museum of Fine Arts was surprising, but college years are flexible. I spent all my time by Praxiteles's Head of Aphrodite. Jill meanwhile did the whole museum, but I was lost in my first feeling of what true beauty is. I have not seen that small luminous piece of marble since I graduated from college, but the memory never pales, any more than do the memories of the star-brimmed sky.

In four years, we did not miss anything in Boston, from the golden birds at Filene's to the robust lobsters at Durgin Park.

This was Boston yesterday. What has happened to the Athens of America? When the news comes on, I tell myself it is the same place, the same sea where the sailing ships came, loaded with spices, teas, silks, and linens. But another school is closed because of rioting, another case of arson is under investigation. A few more murders have just been reported. More corruption will be brought to court. All Boston's history has not been able to protect it from the problems so many modern cities must face.

What started the hate? Who plants the seeds that grow into mammoth poison trees? Why not cut them down as soon as they appear? We who live on Cape Cod can prevent a similar disaster here if we choose men without prejudice to head the governing bodies of the fifteen towns. Already we can see growing seeds of conflict. Build up a few arguments over roads and use of beach buggies, and see how quickly friends become enemies.

Now a good beginning for the coming spring is to erase a few of our personal prejudices. We can start in a very small way by not concentrating on phrases such as "I don't like—." I once met a very pretty young woman at a buffet luncheon given to raise funds for the school playground. I felt sure a natural friendship would ensue. We were introduced over the appetizers.

"I don't like cherry tomatoes," she said. "They have no flavor."

I swallowed mine with no trouble. "There is special Vermont cheese," I said.

"No, thank you," she said. "I don't care for the hard cheeses. Roquefort is my choice."

After we had worked our way down the buffet, I had an encyclopedic list of my companion's dislikes, and I may say

I lost interest before we reached the shrimp. "It's been a pleasure to meet you," I said wistfully.

"Oh, I'll stop in when I go to the Historical Society meeting. That old wooden bridge by Sloane's must be saved."

What a pity we did not begin on our mutual interest in history! Or by explaining to each other how beautiful Cape Cod is.

Who can argue about that?

Saying goodbye to February is not like any other farewell. All month we count the days, and when a whole extra day is added, it is a great pity. But yesterday I was checking the calendar to see how many more weeks we had to struggle through when I heard a familiar sound from the yard. It was my mockingbird. He had just discovered that the thick chunk of ice in the birdbath had melted during the night's rain.

There was *water* again! He swooped down to douse himself. He is such an energetic swimmer I wish he could enter the Olympics; he beats the water with spread wings. Inside of five minutes, the whole bath was filled with birds, and the rim held a circle waiting their turn. The cardinals, who are always aloof, flew from the junipers to sit on the split-rail fence. Only when the first bathers dripped away did the brightest, biggest male drop down to wash and drink. There is a reserve about cardinals that is charming, and their beauty is dazzling, but in summer, if the birdbath is empty, the sound of their scolding brings attention right away.

I forgot the calendar as I looked at a clearing sky, the first in seven days. A bank of blue seal-shaped clouds moved toward Rock Harbor, leaving gentian sky above a silvery Mill Pond. A bevy of buffleheads were busy. I can never hold my breath as long as they do when their heads are under water. But I do not have to dive for my food.

The morning thaw made the air smell of sea and pine and damp earth.

Suddenly I felt that the day was a special gift. I felt like tossing my hat in the air, which was impossible since I do not own a hat. So I opened all the windows to clear the house air.

"February isn't so bad," I told Amber.

"Too cold for tropical paws," she said.

I closed the windows half an hour later, but the freshness still gave a tang to the house.

It was a day that called for something special in the way of supper. And something special arrived only a few minutes later when Jan turned up with a small covered casserole. "Thought you might like a taste of this," she said. "So I made a little extra."

She brought me a steaming bowl.

A purring cat materialized on my lap.

"Whatever it is must be for cats," Amber said.

"Jan, have come coffee and jot down the recipe," I said. And here it is, in Jan's own words. (I'm copying it exactly, from the envelope where she wrote it.)

Scalloped Scallops

Bread crumbs—½ saltines, ½ fresh white bread
A good bunch of parsley
Zap in blender
Melt butter in skillet. Lightly brown crumb mixture. Layer crumbs and scallops (starting with a layer of crumbs) in a buttered casserole. Finish with a layer of crumbs. Pour in enough cream to just come to top (almost). Bake at 400° for about 20 min.

And there you are! Couldn't be easier—or more delicious.

The various night creatures who come for their own February treat at Still Cove don't get anything so elegant. But they never seem to quibble at stale bread, slightly brown apples, and dabs of leftover vegetables. Lately, there has been a new visitor—a large opossum. I've always had skunks and raccoons, but this is my first possum.

People usually say that the possum is ugly, and it's true that he does look like a large rat, with the long snout and naked ears and ratlike tail. But I think my own possum has a certain charm. His face is almost heart-shaped and his little eyes are very bright. When he picks up a piece of bread crust—using his thumb and fingers almost as skillfully as a raccoon does—his little palms are pink and very clean.

I say, "he," but of course this may be a "she." In which case I may be lucky enough to see a backload of babies in a few months. I've read somewhere that opossums have from six to thirteen babies, which have a gestation period of only twelve days and weigh only $\frac{1}{15}$ of an ounce at birth. After birth these thimble-tiny infants manage to work their way into their mother's pouch, where they stay—snug and warm—for about three months. Then they emerge and begin to learn about the outside world as seen from a perch on their mother's back, using their tails to help anchor them securely to her long fur. And that is a sight I would really cherish—a mother opossum ambling over to the feeding dish with thirteen little ones clinging to her back.

Several of the neighbors are also feeding possums these days. Late February is the mating season for many of the small creatures who have been asleep or half asleep all winter. So now, when we talk about greeting the spring robins, we must also welcome these new messengers of the warmer season—the spring possums!

March

March blows in, and the junipers and cedars bend their heads. I like to think it is a welcome. My resident hawk rides on the tallest tip until he sees a possible prey and soars out over Mill Pond. As I sit near the picture window finishing my coffee, I feel a sense of freedom watching him slice the blue air. Although hawks have a bad reputation for raiding hen yards, it does not seem fair to blame a species for struggling to survive, as do we all. That first robin hauling away at an icy worm is not particularly moral, nor is the song sparrow snapping up sunflower seeds. The bouncy bufflehead diving under the water gobbles an innocent fish with no apology.

Bird-watching is one of Amber's favorite occupations. The only bird she ever actually caught was a starling that flew down the chimney. He was as big as she is, but she pounced on him fearlessly. Long after he had been rescued and released outdoors, she paraded back and forth, tail switching, whiskers quivering. Most cats feel that bird-catching is their duty; the instinct goes back to prehistoric times. Amber keeps in practice by chasing moths.

At this time of year, our yard is milling with birds, and sea gulls drop by whenever bread is thrown out. My little red squirrel works his way into the animal-proof bird feeder to gobble enough for a fair-sized raccoon. Every creature senses the change in the season. Even if a light snow is falling, birds, bunnies, and skunks spend more hours out in the open. So do I, putting out more birdseed, checking for the first green tips of crocus.

According to the calendar, spring is supposed to begin on the twenty-first, but nature makes her own decision. The Full Worm Moon moves over Mill Pond around the thirteenth. The name may not sound very romantic, but it reminds us that down in the cold soil the worms are beginning to work their way. Now that we know how important they are, worm farms have been developed. Worms are sold for bait and also to go in gardens, where they do more work than any tool to enrich the earth. Gardeners dig their hands in the soil, and when it is soft and loose they give thanks to the worms.

One certainty about March is that she has her pockets full of winter. The willows wear the pale gold of spring, and the osiers glow; one day it seems that the time has come to let blankets blow on the line. But a day later, snow feathers from a darkening sky.

The other night my friends Gail and Jan quite literally blew in because the strong March wind was at their backs. We sat by the fire sipping hot drinks while Jan's very special scallop soup simmered on the stove.

"This doesn't look like an ordinary snow," I said.

"It's the Sea Snow," Gail said.

"Sea Snow? What's that?"

She settled herself happily. Gail would have been a wonderful teacher. "Well, you know that when moist air from the south reaches a cold front up north, something dramatic is bound to happen. If they meet over water, they make a fog. If they meet over cold land, the mass of fog turns to what is outside your window right now. That's Sea Snow."

"Now I won't have to struggle any more to describe it," I said. "I've tried saying it's like falling waves of fog, dense but not solid. It looks as if you could gather it in handfuls and bring it indoors by the basket. The whole air is pale white. Now I can just say the Sea Snow is here. Incidentally, that's a lovely phrase! We once named a white-and-gold cocker Snow in Summer. But Sea Snow would have been better."

"Soup's on," Jan said. "Will Amber eat scallops?"

Never mind the snow—the next day will bring the first flicker of flame from the swamp maple.

The red-winged blackbirds are on the way!

Sharing special recipes is fun, although copying them out is not. I try to avoid long ones, but my comment when I first tasted Jan's scallop soup was, "I don't care how many things are in this, I want a copy. I'll double it when the granddaughters are here." Actually, it is easy to make, keeps well, will freeze. We like to make a whole supper of it, only adding garlic-toasted rolls.

You need 2 slices diced bacon, 1 cup thinly sliced potatoes, 2 tablespoons butter, 1 pint scallops (bay if possible), 2½ cups water, 1 tablespoon chopped parsley, ½ tablespoon thyme, 1 cup sliced tomatoes, ½ cup cream, 2 tablespoons seasoned bread crumbs, dash of mace.

Cook bacon 2 minutes, set aside. Add butter, scallops, potatoes, parsley, thyme. Sauté 2 minutes, then add water and cover. Cook very slowly for 20 minutes. Do not boil. Add tomatoes; cook 5 more minutes; stir in cream, bacon, crumbs. Sprinkle with mace. Serve in heated bowls.

It should serve 4 to 6, but don't bet on it, because three of us left a tablespoon or so for Amber.

Jan is a meticulous cook, and her recipes are exact about the crucial points. I tend to say, "thyme, parsley, etc., to taste. Simmer until done." But I am careful about "Do not boil." I stand by the stove to count the bubbles.

The wonderful quality of scallop soup is that the seasoned bread crumbs give a creamy texture with no other thickening.

These are available in most groceries and have many uses. As for scallops, they are really the queen of seafood. Eileen DeLory's scallop stew is a perennial favorite in my family and is on the jacket of my last cookbook, and now Jan's scallop soup is a delightful way to present the delicate, savory nuggets from the sea. I like it almost as well as the Scalloped Scallops she introduced me to in February!

Regional recipes were often born in times when food money was scarce and people had to make do with whatever was at hand.

I was reminded of one night during times of financial crisis on the Cape when I was talking to Bobby Gibson.

"I don't worry," Bobby said. "If we have a real depression, I'll hang up my tools and get out my boots and go clamming and scalloping, musseling, catch some flounder. If necessary, go into lobsters. Boots makes fine bread, and the garden has plenty of vegetables. The kids like to pick wild blueberries, huckleberries, blackberries, and beach plums. Nobody has to starve on the Cape."

"It's too bad the Pilgrims didn't realize the bounty nature provided for them right where they first landed," I said.

"They were mostly city people, I guess."

It is true the average Cape income is lower than that inland. And the last working farm in our area was sold some time ago. One must go to the Connecticut valleys to see plump Holsteins ankle deep in rich meadows. But the sandy soil will produce elegant asparagus, strawberries, and moist garden vegetables, including the famous Eastham white turnips, which are a gourmet delicacy. All that is needed is fertilizer for the light soil. Manure is not easy to bring from the barnyard but can be bought, and another gift from the sea is the salt hay which gardeners cherish. Lime, peat moss, and commercial fertilizers are at hand at Snow's, Nickerson's, Gill's.

It is comforting to know the thick rains of March and April

bring nitrogen to the earth, and the sea itself has moisture. And in fall, the killing frost comes late, so homemakers keep canning and freezing until they sigh with relief when the beans stop bearing!

If the oil wells go in, the golden era of Cape Cod will be over; we are sure of that. It seems obvious to everyone but the oil drillers and the government, whose only interest is, apparently, in the possibility of extracting petroleum from the ocean bottom at George's Bank. But Cape Codders are optimistic and still hope the fishing beds may be preserved. This is not only for the Cape itself, but because it furnishes, they say, three fourths of the fish for the nation.

"Something will happen," says the man at the fish market as he lifts a dripping lobster from the tank.

After all, our forefathers did not give up and sail back to England!

The time of sap running is here, when days are warm but nights still cold. At Stillmeadow, our inland farm, thirteen giant sugar maples frame the sky. We used to watch for the dark stream of sap flowing down the massive trunks. This was maple-syrup country, and in March, pails hung all over the valley. At the Stiles farm on the Woodbury road, we could get jars of pale gold "first-run" syrup. That first run is like sunlight. Most of the commercial syrup is second or third run, darker and not so delicate in flavor. The Stiles family has been famous for generations because of their rich, smooth, pure syrup. The old homestead must be full of memories, especially of the days when it was a stage on the underground slave route to Canada. I imagine the refugees set forth filled with New England pancakes and fresh maple syrup.

Sometimes I see a few shining pails, with firm spouts, plugged into sugar maples here on the Cape. And whenever I do, I remember standing in the shed in the Stiles's backyard, where the great vat full of the sweet sap bubbled. And I recall our own efforts to plug the maples at the farm, after I was persuaded that the trees had more than enough syrup to spare. It all sounded very romantic, but we found that we had to get up in the middle of the night to empty the pails, as well as keep a watchful eye on them all day. When the time came to cook down the syrup, we innocently began by boiling the wash kettle of sap on the old iron range in the back kitchen. It was too bad we had just painted the ceiling. The fresh paint peeled off before we even noticed. We also learned that never, never must the sap stop boiling, which meant lugging in logs day and night. After a few days, we took the pails down (you could get special sap buckets, but we had plain tin pails). Gallons and gallons of sticky sap yielded us three small mason jars of syrup.

"It's first run, all right," I said. "We ran day and night."

While deciding just when we would open one of our precious jars, we drove over to the Stiles and came home loaded with enough of their syrup to take care of the family for months. We saved ours for birthday breakfasts and other special occasions.

What the sugar maples are to that area, the cranberry bogs are here on Cape Cod. I am sure that if we had a bog of our own, we would have tried at least once to harvest the rich ruby nuggets. We might have come up with a couple of small jelly glasses of sauce!

I do not believe in generalizations, but like most people, I make them. My current one is that Americans tend to believe they can do anything with or without any training or experience. Farming is an art, raising livestock is a difficult profession, but young families are fleeing to the country in hopes of finding an easy paradise on some small farm. They find instead that apartment living does not teach how to build a good fire in a wood stove or lay out a manageable garden.

Keeping goats is not like coping with subways.

On the Cape, would-be fishermen take off in overloaded boats, minus radios, life jackets, emergency supplies. It is a full-time job for rescuers to haul them in when a quick storm blows up. Even on quiet Mill Pond we see small boats, weighted down to the gunwales, stranded. The motor has died and nobody knows how to start it. In the scramble, one oar floats away. Fortunately, in such a small body of water, someone is sure to cruise by or to park at Town Landing within shouting distance. So even though the newcomers do not bring in a load of bluefish, as my neighbor Pret Barker does, they get back alive.

When I looked out of the kitchen window the other morning, the mammoth oil truck from Snow's was maneuvering around in my small driveway. Paul Underhill was just visible as he slid the canary-yellow monster between the ilex bushes and my cherished oak. Forward, backward again toward the opening for the nozzle (which is behind the juniper). I thought about what those trucks mean to Orleans and to all Cape towns, pumping life into homes, schools, churches, businesses, and to the hospital.

This year, of course, oil is a major preoccupation with the government because of the Mideast crisis. But we go about our affairs with the comfortable feeling that, exactly on time, the oil man will hand us a slip of paper stating that our tanks are filled. This morning I met Paul at the door. In the wild windy weather he looked like a snowman.

"You know, I liked what you said about driving around town," Paul said. "One reason I am so happy with my job is that I drive everywhere—see all the houses, the woods, the water. Keep an eye on everything, the people, the animals, the birds." He grinned as he handed me the slip: 183 gallons. "What's more," he said, "I get paid for doing it. Willie Gallant feels the same way."

"Being happy in your job," I said, "makes life worthwhile."
Which may be a cliché but is still true.

He waved at me as he jumped back into the cab. I heard
no complaints about the hard work—the wind, snow, rain,
sleet, or the narrow roads and difficult driveways like mine.
I had listened to a man who looked for what was good and
enjoyed it thoroughly.

I went back to my dishwashing. What pleasure could possibly be found here? Well, there was the beauty of my thistle-
ware. It was once limited to the British royal family, but I
am sure the Queen never had a chance to dip a piece in
creamy suds, rinse it, and see the soft purple flowers bloom
against the pale blue background. I gently set the plump
little coffee mugs in the dish rack next to the smoothly curved
saucers. Before long there will be crocuses and grape hyacinths to arrange in the little pitcher.

It's good to be reminded every so often that even routine
chores can be rewarding. When I was growing up, we spent
our summers in a cabin in the woods, minus all modern con-
veniences. It was my job to wash the glass lampshades and
trim the wicks. I always felt that it was a deadly chore. But
I did love the clean glow of those lamps at night. The hearth
fire added light as Papa flung on an extra log. While Mama
was mending our clothes, he read aloud—light summer reading such as *The Geological History of North America* or *Commenta-
ries on Vergil*. The Irish setter snuggled as much of himself
as possible in my lap. By then I decided the poems I could
have written earlier in the day if I hadn't had that miserable
lamp cleaning would not have been worth much anyway! I
would do every lamp again in the morning, twice as carefully,
and not complain.

The first Sunday in Lent reminds us that it is time to do
a kind of mental housecleaning. What bad habit can we give
up for Lent—and possibly for good? What can we do to
help others? What new goal can we set for ourselves for

the coming spring? It is always so easy to plan for everyone else and point out other people's weaknesses. Lent is a time for introspection. But I do allow myself to give Amber a suggestion that, for her part, she give up clawing the newly upholstered chair to shreds. But whose fault is it that she needs to have those claws trimmed? Outdoor cats get a natural claw-trimming by scampering up trees, but indoor cats have to work on sofas, drapes, and rugs. My Lenten plan for Amber is really a job for me. It involves either calling Olive to handle the clippers or popping over to Dr. Kim's. Whatever the circumstances, Amber behaves like a tragedy queen but admits she is comfortable afterward—those long, curving needle points are a terrible nuisance.

In March, the geese fly north and mark the calendar for spring. But the little duck pond below my study window has kept a bevy of them here all winter. They managed well except when the water froze over. When only a small area was open water, the pond looked as if it were paved with birds.

Change is in the air, although spring has not yet settled in for good. Sheets flap on clotheslines on bright days (most of us still prefer sun- and wind-dried laundry). After school, yards blossom with children mobile as butterflies now that they have emerged from the chrysalis of snowsuits, mufflers, and mittens. Adults stop chopping wood to get out rakes and pruning shears. A few reckless souls slap fresh paint on the lawn chairs which should have been done in the cellar last winter. (It's really not warm enough to paint.) Stores are more like social clubs than marts.

"How have you been? I just didn't get out—our road was a mess! Now we'll have to get together and catch up."

"Well, you look wonderful. The Lobster Claw will be open April first. Let's meet for lunch."

The Cape as I know it is a social place but lacks the rigid

pressures of so many inland communities. Perhaps the long history of the fisherman's way of life has left an imprint, for his engagements are always based on the weather, the sea, the time when the stripers are running or the bluefish are in.

"Come for dinner Thursday night," is a typical invitation. "Or if Bill has to work late, we'll make it Friday. I'll let you know."

Or it may be a spur-of-the-moment telephone call. "Mark just came in with lobsters. How about supper tonight?"

Sometimes a tradition develops. For years now I have had a standing invitation to Monday-night supper with Millie and Ed. The meal is always substantial, roast beef or a crock of spicy beans, but I look forward just as much to Millie's brisk survey of town news—she has a keen eye and a way with words: I can imagine her as commentator for a TV program called "The Cape Cod Week in Review"—and to Ed's dry humor as we discuss sports or gardening or politics.

Summer is still a long way off, but already the conversation turns to the end of the school year. The small fry will be swept into constant activities, from swimming classes to ballet, scouts to Little League. Teenagers will look for summer jobs, washing dishes, pumping gas, mowing lawns, waiting tables. But how about those leggy youngsters graduating from high school? Where will they go next?

There has been a good deal of talk lately about this generation on Cape Cod. Ours is not an area of great industries, booming factories, big-city business. Family budgets are often tight. The pattern of youth moving steadily from the high school halls of academe to those of ivied colleges is no longer the inevitable course it used to be. Higher education simply costs too much.

"If we had only one child, we would have made it," says a friend. "Four is impossible. There are scholarships, of course, but the amount of a scholarship hasn't kept up with inflation."

One great help here on the Cape is the Community College, which provides two years of excellent training. When I meet some of the faculty members, I long to be able to go back myself for more schooling. Then there is the Technical School which has been needed so long. Students gifted in technical careers can now study on this side of the bridge, instead of giving up all plans for specialized training because inland institutions are out of range. So a beginning has been made.

A second problem for the Cape is said to be the lack of jobs, especially for unskilled young people. Nothing to do, I often hear. I began thinking about this when I first came to Still Cove. There was always work to do at our place for any interested teenager. And none of the boys we came to know ever seemed to feel that they were underprivileged because of growing up on Cape Cod.

Our first helper was ten years old when he tiptoed across the grass to ask if we needed the lawn cut. By the time he began to wrestle with high school English papers, Bobby was part of the family. And while I struggled to explain spelling, he battled with my inability to understand electricity. Meanwhile, he began to get jobs working for carpenters and found his dream. Today he and his wife and two young children live in one of the first houses he built. And every time he is finishing a new home for some very happy owner, he takes me to see it while I still have to skid up planks to get in. They never put in steps until the furniture is due.

Another boy did odd jobs at Still Cove all through high school: ran errands, cleaned the fireplace, delivered groceries. Now Dave is a photographer, covering sports for the newspaper. But I cherish especially the pictures he took of our inland farm during a trip to Connecticut.

My third boy graduated from Nauset only last June. I have already written about Glenn, who is now in the Navy. His graduation picture shows a dark-haired, serious eighteen-year-old in a blue tuxedo, rented at vast expense. I was furious at the thought of his class, most of whom had worked all through school, having to pay so much for suits rented year after year. But he was happy. I described, last January, my feelings when I read his letters. He is a long way from home.

I can go in the bank and who is the man behind the big desk? Bobby's best friend from school. I visit with Stu and Russ Crosby and remember that one of them was in Linda Toomey's class. The Sharkey boy from around the corner is now a big-time lobsterman. So I believe that opportunities are still available on this land reaching out to sea, as well as anywhere in our vast country. But they come only to those who reach.

And how rewarding to find them along with sea, sand dunes, piney woods, clear skies, unpolluted air, and Cape Cod people!

The surf was pounding when Olive and I drove over to Nauset Beach the other day. Under the March wind, huge jade-green waves laced with white heaved and crested and sank back and lifted again. Far out we could see nine snowy gulls bobbing in a row, spaced apart as evenly as if they were part of some artist's design. I've seen the same neat procession in a Japanese print of sand cranes and in the border of an ancient Egyptian wall painting of ducks on the Nile. (Both drawings from the art calendar taped to my kitchen cabinet—my private gallery with regularly changing exhibits.) I'd always thought the painter invented the precise spacing for artistic effect. I see now that it was probably taken direct from Nature (herself an artist with an eye for design).

Every so often we could see a piece of blackened driftwood being carried in by the tide. If my granddaughters, Alice and Anne, had been with us, they would have dashed down to the sea line to look for treasures. When they came back, their windbreaker pockets would have sagged with round pebbles, smooth flakes of purple and white wampum shell, maybe a few bits of frosted sea glass. (They would probably have found a couple of old beer cans, too, which they would bring back for the trash bin.)

I had just been rereading Thoreau's Cape Cod journal that morning, and it seemed as if we might see him at any minute, walking along this same beach—a lean, rangy figure in his brown coat and wide-brimmed black hat. He too found all sorts of prizes on Nauset. Once he waded out to rescue "a valuable cord and buoy, part of a seine, with which the sea was playing." He thriftily took it home to use as a garden line. Another time he found an arrowhead in the sand (how the girls would love that!) and a stone shaped exactly like a large grey clam.

He also found an actual clam, a six-inch sea clam, torn from the bottom by a storm. Around midday, when he took what he called his "nooning" in the shelter of a sandhill, he carved some damp driftwood into shavings, added a few scraps of paper, kindled a small fire, and cooked his clam on the embers. When it was done, one valve held the liquid, the other the meat.

"Though it was very tough," he says, "I found it sweet and savory, and ate the whole with relish. Indeed, with the addition of a cracker or two, it would have been a bountiful dinner." (Alice and Anne might question Thoreau's rather Spartan definition of a bountiful dinner, but they would agree that clams should be part of it.)

Somewhat later an old oysterman told him that although the great clams were good to eat, it was important to take out the poisonous part first. "People say it would kill a cat," the old man added. Remembering his lunch, Thoreau decided that he was tougher than a cat.

That evening, however, Thoreau changed his mind. "I began to feel the potency of the clam which I had eaten, and I was obliged to confess to our host that I was no tougher than the cat he told of." They were thinking of country cats, of course, who could digest boot leather, not delicate eaters like my own Amber.

Thoreau was pleased to read later that the Pilgrims had had the same experience with what they called "great muscles." It brought him nearer to the Pilgrims, he says, "to be thus reminded by a similar experience I was so like them."

It did not dampen his enthusiasm for investigating unexpected beach finds, either. The next day he came across a bottle, covered with barnacles, partly buried in the sand, "All that remained I fancied from the wreck of a rowdy world." The cork was still tight and the bottle half full of red ale, "which still smacked of juniper," he reports with satisfaction. This time, luckily, his tasting had no ill effects.

Thoreau was also fascinated by the tales fishermen told him. "You might make a curious list of articles which fishes have swallowed—sailors' open clasp-knives, and bright tin snuff boxes, not knowing what was in them—and jugs, and jewels, and Jonah." (Is he joking here that a fish might reject snuff tins if it knew what they contained? You can't always tell with Thoreau. His straight-faced Yankee humor is sometimes easy to miss.)

Thoreau includes in his journal a newspaper clipping about a sixty-pound rockfish in whose stomach was found a certificate of membership in the Methodist Episcopal Church, wet and crumpled but still legible.

My thoughts of the visitor from Walden came to an end when Olive spoke up.

"Getting dark, how about heading home for a hot drink by the fire?"

"Good idea," I said. "And Amber will be getting hungry."

So we turned inland again, leaving the empty beach to the waves and the gulls and a certain tall, shadowy figure.

A call came today from Mary Anne, one of the nurses I met last fall. "Just calling to say hello," she said. I have been in the hospital several times in the last year or so, and each time my stay has been lightened by unexpected gestures: a busy doctor took time to stand at the foot of the bed and discuss books, a nurse lingered to ask about the family snapshots taped to the wall, a young man with a mop offered to bring coffee from the canteen down the hall. I knew that I could count on help from family and friends, but these other moments were a surprise gift. When I went home to Still Cove, I took with me not only a renewed lease on health but also some special memories.

"Dear March—Come in—" Emily Dickinson says in one of my favorite poems.

> How glad I am—
> I hoped for you before—
> Put down your Hat—
> You must have walked—
> How out of Breath you are—
> Dear March, how are you . . . ?

And of course, as always, Emily is right. March does arrive like a sudden visitor, breathless and rushed. And we do feel, especially here in New England, that we've been waiting a long time. I wonder about the hat, though. My own picture of March is closer to Hal Borland's; he says that March is tousled and has muddy shoes. Not the hat-wearing sort.

Certainly there is a sense of hurry about this month. Only last week, it was winter. Tiny Tim left feathery footprints on the snowy fence rail; the birdbath was solid crystal. Mill Pond was agate green under a grey sky, and the ducks huddled together near the shore as if they were trying to keep warm. If the sun came out, everything glittered, but otherwise, the view from my window was dark even at midday.

Whenever someone opened the door, the icy air knifed

in and Amber shivered in spite of her fur. I kept my blue crocheted shawl and an extra sweater handy.

What's more, it began to seem as if winter would just keep going, right into May. Nature was making up for the mild weather we had during the earlier months. Maybe this year we would miss the crocuses and the first daffodils altogether and have ice fringing the cedars until lilac season.

Then, overnight, everything changed. It was exactly overnight, too. We went to bed in winter. We woke up to spring. Blowy, muddy, full of energy—March arrived. And spring came too.

This morning the sky looks scrubbed and clean, and the wind is sending scurries of ripples flashing back and forth across Mill Pond. The gulls are shouting and somewhere in the bushes there's a small bird—which I can't locate and so can't identify—chirping what is definitely a spring song. (It's not one of the familiar songs. Maybe this is a newcomer. Whoever it is sounds happy as a lark—or happy as any spring bird.)

Before long we will be able to throw open all the windows and let the March air pour through the house. Not quite yet, though. I'll still keep a warm wrap near at hand for a week or two more. And I'll still wake up at night and listen to make sure the furnace is purring steadily away in the cellar. The little house creaks and rustles comfortably.

Unless there is a wind, the world outside is very silent on a cold night. But the house talks softly to itself. The heat flowing out of the wall vents makes a different sound in every room. I think I could be taken blindfolded into any room of the house and know at once where I was just by listening.

The main vent in the living room hisses gently like a kettle (not the whistling kind, a regular enamel tea kettle). In the blue bathroom, there is a steady hum. Something flutters when the vents in the wing are going—could there be a few twigs or a spray of dried oak leaves in the pipes somewhere? In my bedroom, there is a little pop and crackle every so often. Then, when the furnace turns itself off, the whole house reacts. It sounds exactly as if someone were tiptoeing from room to room. This house is too young to have a ghost, so I think what I hear is the sound of the walls and floors murmuring and settling as the warm air flow stops. "Cold outside tonight." "Snug enough in here."

I mentioned this to my granddaughter Anne when she phoned yesterday, and she had a different theory.

"Do you know the song called 'The Sound of Silence,' Gram? Maybe that's what you're hearing."

Whatever the explanation, I love the small, domestic noises of the nighttime. (The sound of mice in the walls or squirrels in the attic would be something else again. Luckily, I do *not* hear anything like that.) No chance of feeling lonely when the house itself has so much to say!

Amber ignores house sounds, but when the March wind raps at the window she wakes from her nap and stares disapprovingly in the direction of the noise. Then she turns that golden gaze on me.

"Why do you put up with it?" she wants to know. "Can't you do something about all this banging around?"

I think again of Emily Dickinson's poem:

Who knocks? That April.

I reach for Amber's brush. In April she will be able to put on her leash and go outdoors to investigate the new grass.

"Be patient," I tell her. "It won't be long."

The March columns are the last
that Gladys Taber wrote. She died
on March 11, 1980.

223